CRITICAL
Minds and
DISCERNING
Hearts

CRITICAL Minds and DISCERNING Hearts

A Spirituality of Multicultural Teaching

Kathleen T. Talvacchia

CHALICE PRESS

ST. LOUIS, MISSOURI

Bible quotations, unless otherwise noted, are from the *New Revised Standard Version Bible*, copyright 1989, Division of Christian Education of the National Council of the Churches of Christ in the United States of America. Used by permission. All rights reserved.

Cover art: © PhotoDisc, Inc.
Cover and interior design: Elizabeth Wright

This book is printed on acid-free, recycled paper.

Visit Chalice Press on the World Wide Web at
www.chalicepress.com

10 9 8 7 6 5 4 3 2 1   03 04 05 06 07 08

Library of Congress Cataloging–in–Publication Data

Talvacchia, Kathleen T.
    Critical minds and discerning hearts : a spirituality of multicultural teaching / Kathleen T. Talvacchia.
        p. cm.
    Includes bibliographical references.
    ISBN 0-8272-0491-4 (alk. paper)
    1. Multicultural education. 2. Teaching. 3. Critical pedagogy. I. Title.
    LC1099.T35 2003
    370.117—dc21

                                                                2002007781

Printed in the United States of America

Contents

Acknowledgments

I imagine that any number of feelings might be present at the completion of a book project—elation, satisfaction, anxiety, relief. As I finish this work, I am left with a profound feeling of gratitude. This book was difficult to conceive and yet utterly instinctive to write. Its creation revealed to me what I have always believed about experiential learning: professional wisdom comes from the quality of the reflection on the work. I have sought to be as honest as possible in my own reflection and to subject my teaching and learning experiences to the same critical mind and discerning heart that I was advocating. I feel tremendous gratitude for the grace to face the challenge.

I would like to thank all who supported me in this process. First, I wish to thank The Wabash Center for Teaching and Learning in Theology and Religion, who supported this text with a generous research grant in 1999 that allowed me to complete its first draft. Katie Bergin served marvelously as my research assistant at that time and provided helpful feedback on the first draft. I also wish to thank Union Theological Seminary for its support of the manuscript revision during my sabbatical in the spring and summer of 2001.

Many colleagues read all or part of the manuscript and provided many helpful comments and incisive critical feedback: Victor Anderson, Angela Bauer, Mary Boys, David Carr, Ana María Díaz-Stevens, Charles Foster, Brigitte Kahl, Barbara Lundblad, Irene Monroe, When-in Ng, Evelyn Parker, Stephanie Paulsell, Daniel Schipani, Ann Ulanov, Janet Walton, and Jace Weaver.

I wish to thank the many friends who provided love and support in the process: Elizabeth Carl, Susan Davies, David

McDonagh, Sandra Jones, Jae-won Lee, Irma Levesque, Mary Christine O'Connor, Steve Thomsen, and Karen Wood. Special thanks go to Susan Blain for her care and concern, especially in the early writing of this work.

My family has been a wonderful support to me and unfailingly believed in me and my project, even when I had doubts myself: Bruno and Connie Talvacchia, Judy Talvacchia and John Boll, John and Ruth Talvacchia, Bette Talvacchia, Mary Lynn and Dave Barr, Janet Talvacchia, and Marie and Pete Nuzzo. My nephews and nieces are always a joy to me: Matthew, Jed, Mark, Catherine, Elizabeth, Mary Frances, and David. I wish to remember especially my mother, Bess Merola Talvacchia (1920–1978), whose life and death gave me a solid foundation for a discerning mind and a critical heart. Finally, I wish to thank Su Yon Pak, friend, colleague, and intellectual provocateur, to whom this work is dedicated with love and affection.

Introduction

Teaching in a Diverse World

It is not that the world has become multicultural. We have always been a world of pluralistic cultures and peoples. The change that has happened is that now we accept the reality of that pluralism as a norm and a value that we have not before. The dominance of a universal voice that Audre Lorde termed "the mythical norm"[1] struggles to be overthrown, as new and diverse points of view become part of the world's religious, social, political, and educational conversations. The world is becoming inescapably connected and interactive with a plurality of peoples, ideas, and contexts.

As teachers we struggle to understand how to teach well in the diverse society and educational contexts in which we increasingly find ourselves. Even if we teach in a more or less monocultural environment, can we say that we are educating well if we do not expose our students to a variety of cultures, social groups, and ideas? This diversity is often a highly contested and conflictual experience. Embracing pluralism often means embracing shifting sands of change where there was once a rock of solid certainty. Teaching in such a context can often be a combination of exhilaration and terror. In our best moments, the conflicts are over important ideas and actions that come to

1

a new and more workable expression through negotiation. In our worst moments, we are stuck in intractable problems that foment resentment, violence, and rage. How are we to function as effective teachers in this complicated context?

These are some of the questions I bring to the writing of this text. For the past twenty years that I have been a teacher, I have struggled to understand the complicated dynamic between Christian ethical norms of solidarity with the disenfranchised and the concrete process of learning how to live out that ethical requirement. This book represents my own explorations into understanding this difficult dynamic and finding a way to function both morally and effectively as a teacher. I believe that the most important skill one can bring to the teaching ministry, besides strong intelligence and excellent communication abilities, is an emotional and mental agility— one that is able to comprehend the nuances of multiple relationships. I hope in this text to share with you some of the struggles and successes I have had in this teaching journey, and how I have come to understand them as part and parcel of teaching well.

This book does not explicitly answer the question of how we should teach in a multiculturally diverse context. Rather, it explores the understandings of mind and the habits of heart that I have come to see as imperative for this most important work of teaching. It is, in effect, a spirituality of teaching in a context of radical diversity.

In many ways my life experience has focused me in the direction of untangling the confusing mass of issues that diversity presents. I grew up in an urban context of diverse cultures, ethnicities, and races in Philadelphia. My family culture was proudly ethnic, refusing as Italian Americans to fully assimilate into the dominant Protestantism and Anglo-Saxon culture of the United States. I have struggled as a feminist in the Roman Catholic Church—a Vatican II child in a church pulling back from the reform energies of that important movement in church history. I have been a professional lay minister in an overly clericalized church. When I came out as a lesbian, in addition to contending with the homophobia and heterosexism of society, I contended with a faith community that could not understand my lesbian orientation and a gay and lesbian community that could not accept my religious orientation and values. Like many of us, I have personally lived many differences that have significant social and political consequences.

Many years in the context of Union Theological Seminary in New York City also influenced the questions of this work. I spent six years as a graduate student and two years as an administrator in the academic office in the area of Student Life and Field Education, and since 1994 I have been a member of the faculty in Ministry and Theology. From this context and the varying roles that I have had in it, I have come to understand the complexities of a diverse academic community and the constructive and destructive types of conflicts that it engenders. The academic rigor of the Union context, combined with its openly contentious struggles to live out a just social order, has sharpened my questions, deepened my analyses, and challenged every fiber of my being to be faithful to my ethical commitments and to embody them in what I say as well as in what I do. It has also been profoundly exhilarating. Discovering more effective ways of living morally in a diverse world is a major satisfaction of working in such an environment. I often remind myself (and others at the seminary) of an important reality: It is not that there is a solution already in existence that will assist us in negotiating the necessary conflicts that social structural difference and diversity impose, one that we are refusing to implement. Rather, we are creating in our struggles a blueprint that we can bring to our work in the world. It is the profound work of co-creation with God and prophetic reimagining forming new models of community in a pluralistic world. We are discovering ways to live in diversity that respect difference and foster just relationships.

Connecting these educational insights with these personal experiences in diverse contexts, I have wondered about what connections there might be between a heightened sensitivity to understanding the experiences of privilege and marginalization within social groups and an enhanced ability to act in solidarity with those who suffer the effects of the structural discrimination present in an unjust social order. Most significantly, I have sought to understand how these habits of heart and mind might become a fundamental aspect of a teacher's identity, practice, and spiritual formation. These issues are important to me because I understand teaching as a ministry, that is, a service to others in the name of God. For my personal integrity as a teacher, it is fundamentally important that what I teach and the way I teach cohere, that intellectual content and pedagogical process correlate. How can I teach about justice if I teach unjustly?[2]

A grounding assumption of this work is that we can more effectively teach in ways that promote social justice when we begin to understand experiences of marginalization that are the lived reality of groups other than ourselves. Also, we can understand our own experiences of marginalization or privilege in relation to the experience of others. This involves developing a multicultural sensitivity that is a habit of mind and heart rather than a form of political correctness.

Multiculturally Sensitive Pedagogy Is Not Political Correctness

Some might cynically see the attempt to develop a more multiculturally sensitive pedagogy as an exercise in developing "political correctness" for teaching. Nothing could be further from the truth. Rather, a multiculturally sensitive pedagogy attempts to develop a spiritual sensitivity that allows us to see those we teach more fully and completely as human beings, and thereby meet their learning needs more effectively. As a way of explaining this more clearly, it is important to understand what a multiculturally sensitive pedagogy is *not*.

- It is not "political correctness" or some way of giving an illogical advantage to one group over another all in the name of an uncritical ideology or political stance.
- It is not an unthinking adherence to a political stance. It has clear commitments and understands that no education is neutral. It does not sacrifice critical thinking in order to maintain its ideological purity.
- It is not the avoidance of conflict or challenge with discriminated-against groups all in the name of supportive advocacy.
- It is not pandering to a marginalized group in the name of gaining the moral high ground for the purposes of manipulation.
- It is not uncritically changing teaching techniques because they are thought to be better for various groups of students or because they are the hot or latest pedagogical trend.
- It is not adding cultural diversity to a paradigm designed by the dominant culture without critically examining the dominant paradigm.[3]

Rather, a multiculturally sensitive pedagogy is a conviction and an ethical orientation that a teacher brings to a teaching context that grounds pedagogical action and instructional technique. The conviction believes in empowerment for all students in the learning process and an understanding that all can learn when the content is made relevant to their experiences and is critically reflected upon. The conviction emphasizes justice in the social order and equity in the educational system as a moral necessity of a good society.

Multiculturally Sensitive Pedagogy Is a Habit of Mind and Heart

Just as it was important to distinguish what a multiculturally sensitive pedagogy is not, it is also important to clarify what it is.

- It owns up to its point of view; that is, it is overt in its ideological orientation. By not recognizing that it has an ideological point of view embedded in it, monocultural pedagogy obscures its biases in a false notion of universalism. Multiculturally sensitive pedagogy understands that worldview and experience affect content, learning, and comfort level in class. As pedagogy, it is openly concerned with creating a just and accessible learning environment for the diversity of students that are in a class. It recognizes that both course content and teachers who organize that content have an interpretation that privileges some persons and creates obstacles for others. It actively seeks to make course content accessible to all groups.
- It is a critical thinking awareness about the reality of social structural marginalization and disempowerment, and the way that this reality affects the learning process. It is an awareness of social power, and disenfranchisement from that power.
- It is a spiritual stance that one brings to the teaching activity. It is a quality of relationship to humanity in general and to specific human persons in community, rooted in a sense of justice and fairness according to God's desire for human beings.
- It is a conversion process whereby our understanding of someone who is "other" to us (because he or she has a different experience of life and social institutions) is challenged by a genuine awareness of the reality of prejudice and social structural discrimination in the lived experience of that person.

A multiculturally sensitive pedagogy is essential for those from the dominant culture. However, even within socially marginalized groups, social structural power differences exist. The dynamics of racism, sexism, classism, heterosexism, ageism, ableism, just to name a few, have an interlocking nature. One can be discriminated against as a person of color and experience male privilege within that social grouping. Multiculturally sensitive pedagogy recognizes the interstructural aspects of social oppression and their reality in many social contexts. It resists the simplistic dichotomies of hegemony and privilege and understands social structural issues in their nuance.

Changing Understanding

My personal motivation and influences, as well as my understanding of what a multiculturally sensitive pedagogy looks like and does not look like, form the thesis of this book. I hope to show that, from the perspective of being a member of the dominant culture in a social context, the spirituality of multicultural teaching entails *changing our understanding about those who are "other" to us, rather than merely changing our teaching techniques.* Changing our teaching techniques without a changed understanding opens teachers to the danger of an unthinking political correctness that stops conversation and ultimately patronizes marginalized groups. It demands a spiritual conversion that entails attentiveness to the experiences of those who live the reality of marginalization, as well as a commitment to stand with socially targeted groups and work with them in their empowerment.

What does it mean to change our understanding about those who are other to us? It means that we must make every effort to get to know what they experience in life and how those experiences are different from our own. Specifically, it means learning from another what his or her experiences of privilege and marginalization are, and letting that awareness challenge our awareness of ourselves, of others, and of social groupings. The experience of contradiction between what should be just human interaction and what is in reality an unjust social structure promotes a critical thinking process that can then be combined with a compassionate response. Head and heart, thinking and feeling, combine to create a response toward others that listens to their needs and acts in solidarity with them in their empowerment.

One of the genuine problems of attempting to teach in diverse contexts is that the mistakes we make have consequences that involve whole persons and their existential realities. When we as teachers fail to understand, for example, the racial isolation that an African American student experiences in an all-white classroom, we do not just create potential harm to that student's ability to learn. We are unwittingly participating in yet another experience of racial discrimination that adds to the accumulated load the person bears. Our actions affect the person's existential reality. The whole person gets taken into consideration when we use a multiculturally sensitive pedagogy.

There are many ways that our attempts to teach in diverse contexts fail. At times we do not understand something about the culture with which we are dealing. Perhaps we unintentionally offend. Perhaps we are defensive when our mistake is pointed out to us, thereby compounding the relational distance between the student and ourselves. To teach in a diverse context demands unrelenting honesty, intelligence, emotional sensitivity, and humility. We must be willing to see our mistakes, seek forgiveness from those we have offended, and learn to forgive ourselves.

Knowledge of self separates teachers who truly communicate with their students from those who merely impart information to be digested. Teaching essentially involves an action of vulnerability because we present the content to be learned through the vehicle of ourselves. Who we are as persons never separates from our teaching selves. Parker Palmer speaks to this point eloquently when he says, "We teach who we are."[4] For Palmer, teaching emerges from one's inner self, and therefore, as we teach, we project the condition of our souls onto our students, the subject matter, and classroom interactions. Without this inner knowledge of self, we risk our teaching becoming a self-serving project in which we use teaching to shore up our own fragile egos. In this situation we can become less concerned about how well our students are learning and more concerned about how our students make us look professionally.

Palmer's work focuses on the centrality of the "inner landscape" of a teacher's life. He believes that "good teaching cannot be reduced to technique; good teaching comes from the identity and integrity of the teacher."[5] I think that Palmer rightly highlights it as an absolutely fundamental aspect of teaching. Knowing who we are as people and having integrity in that identity grounds us in confidence and self-assurance in our work with others. We are able to attend to our own ego needs without imposing that need on our students. Teaching demands a profound de-centering of self so that we can attend to the learning needs of our students.

This is especially true in a multiculturally sensitive pedagogy. In a diverse teaching context, teachers must know about and be able to communicate with a variety of persons from diverse backgrounds and experiences. Included in that context is our own social location and particularity. Our own identity in gender, race, ethnicity, economic class, or sexual orientation has a tremendous effect on classroom dynamics, for we are the ones who have responsibility for the class experience. As teachers in multicultural settings, we must have knowledge of ourselves as persons and as members of a larger social group. But we must also know our students in their particularity as persons *and* as members of social groups. This is an important shift in thinking from a monocultural teaching environment to a multicultural one. In a culturally diverse learning context teachers need to know themselves and their students in two ways: as individuals and as members of communities that have different experiences in society because of prejudice and discrimination. Students' lived experiences as individuals must be seen in the context of their social location within an unjust society that privileges some groups and creates obstacles for others.

Attentiveness: The Process of Forming
Critical Minds and Discerning Hearts

A multiculturally sensitive pedagogy demands of teachers the ability to see ourselves as teachers and those we teach in a complex reality: uniqueness as persons *and* particularity of experience as members of a social identity grouping. This is an aspect of the spirituality of multicultural teaching that must be understood clearly. In order to teach effectively in a diverse context, teachers need a spirituality that engages both critical social analysis and empathetic sensitivity. In short, a spirituality of multicultural teaching demands that teachers form themselves with *critical minds,* capable of seeing the social structural realities of society and their effects on learners, and *discerning hearts,* capable of viewing each person as an individual who has hopes, dreams, aptitudes, skills, fears, insecurities, and scars. The spirituality of multicultural teaching involves attentiveness to the twin realities of social discrimination and personal and group resistance to it. It is this combination of critical thinking and discerning compassion that marks teachers who are ready to engage the complexity as well as the rewards of teaching in diverse contexts.

The substance of this book engages the process of forming teachers with critical minds and discerning hearts who are capable of teaching effectively in multicultural contexts. I believe that this formation is achieved through a series of reflective experiences on ourselves and on those who are other to us in varying ways. Rather than viewing them as a sequential progression of steps, I prefer to think of them as dialogical movements of experiences that we reflect on theologically. There are many ways into the habits of heart and mind that this work suggests; however, I do think that these movements are essential as holistic elements of a multicultural pedagogy. They are a kind of dialogic process of action and reflection that hopefully leads us as teachers to greater wisdom about teaching in diverse contexts. These reflective experiences are grounded in a spiritual stance of attentiveness that forms the core of a critical mind and a discerning heart effectively in multicultural contexts.

Clarifying Terms

Several important ideas ground the perspective this work takes in understanding teaching in a diverse world. First, while there are ethical convictions that inform the commitments guiding this text, it seeks primarily to articulate a spirituality able to animate one's pedagogy. By spirituality I mean a soul force energy that connects and relates human beings to the Divine, self, and community. Here, I am influenced by Parker Palmer's notion of examining the "inner landscape of the teaching self" in which he reflects on three "pathways" to chart that landscape: intellectual, "the way we think about teaching and learning"; emotional, "the way we and our students feel as we teach and learn"; and spiritual, "the diverse ways we answer the heart's longing to be connected to the largeness of life."[6]

Second, this work understands multicultural education as an approach to teaching and learning that respects cultural pluralism in an interdependent and global world. Multicultural education understood as such criticizes educational perspectives and educational systems that ignore the reality of this diversity and the overt or covert issues of dominance and marginalization that are endemic to it. In this way I situate myself theoretically in that educational perspective.[7]

I have found Christine Bennett's definition of multicultural education useful for establishing the parameters of this perspective. She defines multicultural education in the United States as

> an approach to teaching and learning that is based upon democratic values and beliefs, and affirms cultural pluralism within culturally diverse societies and an interdependent world. It is based on the assumption that the primary goal of public education is to foster the intellectual, social, and personal development of virtually *all* students to their highest potential.

Multicultural education is comprised of four interactive dimensions: the movement towards equity, curriculum reform, the process of becoming interculturally competent, and the commitment to combat prejudice and discrimination, especially racism.[8]

This definition has several helpful characteristics that influence this work. It affirms cultural diversity as opposed to cultural assimilation. It values education as a way to empower all students in society. It grounds the work of multicultural education in several concrete tasks: providing equity in educational contexts, reforming curriculum, developing skills for intercultural competence, and combating prejudice. It views the issue of prejudice broadly without losing a sense of the centrality of racism in our diverse society. While this book does not explicitly deal with the issues raised in the definition, my agreement with its basic tenets informs my approach to multicultural teaching.

Pluralism as a response to the actuality of a diverse and interdependent world comprises a third grounding idea in this work. Diana Eck's helpful explication of the nuances of pluralism influences my understanding of the issue greatly.[9] While she speaks primarily in the context of religious pluralism, her comments are useful for understanding the issue as a broader reality in a society with multiple diversities. She highlights five characteristics toward a practical understanding of pluralism. For the purposes of this book, however, the first two points are the most significant.

First, "pluralism is not the sheer fact of plurality alone, but is active engagement with plurality."[10] Making the point that plurality and pluralism are not the same, she challenges us to understand that diversity must be engaged for it to be genuine pluralism. In many classrooms, teachers are often greeted with *de facto* cultural diversity. How we interact with that plurality makes all the difference for effective multicultural teaching.

Second, she states, "pluralism is not simply tolerance, but also the seeking of understanding."[11] Tolerance might allow coexistence, but it does nothing to assist in mutual understanding and the ability to live together in community. Because tolerance does not require one to recognize or comprehend another, it can be a genuine obstacle to constructive engagement. Effective multicultural teaching seeks a classroom in which students create a learning community of mutual understanding and constructive engagement.

Eck's understanding of pluralism as involving active participation with those who are other to us that goes beyond mere tolerance resonates with my deepest convictions about multicultural teaching. As teachers in a diverse classroom, we commit ourselves to creating learning environments in which all students can feel taken seriously, understood in their social milieu, and respected in their uniqueness.

Finally, my commitment to reflect on a *spirituality* of multicultural teaching represents my understanding of the importance of teachers' ability to care for themselves so that they may better care for the educational empowerment of their students. In this sense I am influenced by bell hooks' articulation of an "engaged pedagogy" whereby teachers "must be actively committed to a process of self-actualization that promotes their own well-being if they are to teach in a manner that empowers their students."[12] Rather than an excuse to be self-absorbed, an engaged pedagogy understands that no teachers can empower students if they are themselves disempowered from burnout, despair, or exhaustion. Being well grounded and whole as a human being assists our ability to relate to our students as whole persons. Multicultural teaching succeeds best in a holistic environment into which both teacher and learner can bring themselves and their experiences without evasion or fear.

Audience and Structure of the Book

As a work concerned with a spiritual approach to multicultural teaching, this book would be useful to teachers in both church and school contexts. In many ways, the spiritual grounding in understanding those who are other to us is pertinent in either teaching context. However, I draw greatly on my own teaching practice that has been primarily in the area of higher education of adults, mostly in a school setting.[13] Those readers who teach in colleges, universities, or seminaries might find the most connection with the reflections and examples in the text.

Because the spirituality of multicultural teaching encompasses head and heart, analysis and feeling, the structure of the book follows an integrative, action-reflection process. I make use of critical incidents, an educational tool for uncovering assumptions and acknowledging the emotionality of learning. Stephen Brookfield describes critical incidents as "brief written reports compiled by students about their experience of learning."[14] These learnings are the ones that stand out in a learner's experience, either positively or negatively. Critical incidents foster analysis of these experiences in concrete, contextually specific ways that can serve to highlight the possible contradictions between the assumptions that one brings into a learning context and the realities of what is present.[15] Each chapter begins with a critical incident from my teaching experience in a multicultural context, which I reflect on in order to perceive the deeper pedagogical and theological issues present. This structure is intentional on my part. I seek to model in this process the type of spiritual and theological reflection on teaching practice that teachers must engage in for effective pedagogy in a multicultural context.

It is my hope that readers will bring to this work their own reflections and experiences of multicultural teaching. To that end each chapter will have a brief study-reflection on teaching and study questions that I hope will allow readers to engage their own teaching practices in a spiritually thoughtful manner. While these questions can be engaged individually, they are best engaged in conversation with colleagues, mentors, and others who support our work as teachers and who help us to be critically honest with ourselves. Teaching is a reflected-upon practice.[16] We become more capable teachers only through the action of reflection. A deep, integrated reflection on teaching practices necessarily involves reflection on our inner selves. These reflections are designed to help facilitate our formation as teachers in diverse contexts.

One final word about the point of view taken in this text: I wish to avoid the simplistic dichotomies of male/female, white/black, rich/poor, gay/straight that are such an enormous problem in discussion of multicultural realities. Such dichotomies erase the real differences that exist cross-culturally and intra-culturally in social groups. The complexity of teaching in a multicultural context is a result, in part, of the varied relationships of dominance and subordination that we have to one another in an unjust social structure. For example, a Hispanic man may have some measure of institutional power as teacher, but the reality of prejudice in the larger context of society diffuses that institutional power. The social power of persons of color in an institutional setting always exists within the larger power relations in a society. Similarly, women of color share with men of color the experience of racism, but they experience also the reality of sexism from society as a whole as well as within their own communities.

Awareness of these complex relationships, and the ways in which they operate in the pedagogical process, challenges us as teachers. The spirituality of teaching in a diverse context involves openness to learning these relationships in the rough-and-tumble interaction of pedagogical practice. It involves openness to learning in the action-reflection of the teaching process.

This book engages my own experience as a teacher/learner who struggles to learn ways to teach better in various contexts. It is a journey that I love and find deeply challenging and gratifying. It is my ministry in the world, my vocational calling to service in the world in the name of God. My reflection on this vocational journey is part of my identity as a teacher, an aspect of how I have come to know who I am and what I am called to do in this world.

Reflection on Teaching Practice

What are the ways in which we already bring a critical mind and a discerning heart into our teaching? What resources do we already possess that can aid us in our attempts to teach effectively in multicultural contexts?

These are some of the questions that are important to begin with in our own study and analysis of our teaching practice. One resource we have is the way that we *image* the activity of teaching. In a class on teaching practices, a student explained her image of teaching in the following way: "learning to walk with one's mind in her heart."[17] This is a marvelous image of teaching with a critical mind and a discerning heart. It implies that the act of teaching is profoundly intellectual—one cannot teach well without some serious thinking about subject matter, audience, and pedagogical design.[18] But it also makes clear that good teaching demands sensitivity to people and the concerns that they bring into the learning environment. This agility becomes an essential skill for multicultural teaching contexts, for it demands that the teacher understand the multiplicity of relationships that are present in the group on both the personal and social structural level.

The image also shows that teaching involves doing— "walking" with both head and heart. Teaching is an embodied action. We cannot teach in the abstract, just as we cannot learn to teach in theory. And because it is embodied and deals with real people, the mistakes we make can be very problematic. Therefore, the image also involves "learning" to do it more effectively. Multicultural contexts heighten the existing vulnerability of teaching. The embodiment of teaching occurs in an enormously complicated interpersonal space. Teachers need to bring all of their knowledge and intelligence, but also their wisdom about communication and relationships.

Questions for study and reflection:

1. What is your image of teaching? What is your image of teaching in a multicultural context? Are the images the same or different? Why?
2. How would you finish the following statement? Teaching in a diverse context is like _____.
3. What is your definition of teaching? What aspects of it are useful for a multicultural context? What aspects are not useful? Why?

1

Perceptive Attentiveness

Forming Critical Minds and Discerning Hearts

When I was a graduate student, I participated in a study-immersion tour in 1991 to Brazil, with visits to Rio de Janeiro, São Paulo, and Salvador in the Bahia region. This experience, so important to understanding myself as both teacher and learner, provides an appropriate starting point for an exploration into the spirituality of multicultural teaching.

This was my first visit to a "Third World" country, and I found myself feeling deeply convicted about the contradictions that I was seeing. One cannot view the injustices of global economic inequity without extending a judgment to "First World" countries in general, and the United States in particular. I saw vividly my own privilege in comparison to the extreme poverty that exists for the majority of Brazilians.

Toward the end of the tour our group met with a Brazilian woman who organized female prostitutes in Rio de Janeiro. As she spoke, it became very clear that she understood prostitution differently than we did. Coming from our group's mostly white, middle-class experience (although not entirely), many experienced discomfort at her comfortable acceptance of prostitution as a viable profession for poor Brazilian women. She spoke about the limited options available to women without education or job skills. She had worked in a factory for a period of time, enduring what she described as long hours, minimal pay, and dehumanizing working conditions. I struggled with her words, thinking, "Doesn't she see the male exploitation of women that she is promoting? Why is she participating in her own oppression? Doesn't she see that prostitution is inherently immoral?" It was clear I did not understand enough about the realities of the poverty of many Brazilian women.[1]

Clearly, I had some knowledge of Brazil, both through the experiences of the trip and through preparatory reading, that I could bring to this situation. Yet I still found myself struggling to listen and understand the context of discrimination, poverty, and limited choices within which this woman lived. Part of the intention of this study-immersion tour was the expectation that precisely such global learning experiences would positively influence our own teaching. Yet I was caught exactly where I did not want to be: a white, middle-class woman from the United States passing judgment on a woman from a completely different social location and context.

I struggled to find a way to see the situation more openly and with less reactive judgment. For me, the significant moment focused around my question about the "inherent immorality" of prostitution. Suddenly, I realized as I sat there that this type of judgment had often been leveled at me as a lesbian woman. I immediately felt in my heart the pain of that judgment. The significance of this insight was so vividly clear that I almost exclaimed aloud! I was doing to the speaker what had been done to me. I had the experience of being met with preexisting judgments from people about the morality of a lesbian orientation and life, without those people really bothering to hear my story or get to know me.

Suddenly, I heard this woman's story with new ears. I began to hear the speaker articulate the limitations forced on the choices of Brazilian women by poverty, sexism, and United States economic imperialism, and how prostitution becomes a viable economic choice that gives women financial means and some measure of control over their bodies and working conditions. In the end, the speaker made it clear that if she had a choice, she would still remain a prostitute, for she loved the company of the women with whom she worked.

As I later reflected on this insight, I realized that my own experience of discrimination, and the pain that I have experienced from it, opened me up to hear the speaker's story in a way that I could not before. As a woman I have experienced patriarchal discrimination in my own context. I know about the limited choices that patriarchy imposes on me. I tried to understand how this might be *even more the case* given her very different social location. I also know about the dynamics of discrimination on a social structural level from my experiences as both female and lesbian. I realized that this knowledge, on both a cognitive and affective level, helped me to hear the speaker's story with greater empathy and understanding.

It also made clear to me what I did not know about her context. While I knew about patriarchal discrimination, I did not know how it functioned in the Brazilian context. Nor was I able to fully understand the combination of racism, sexism, and poverty that were part of her reality. While I could comprehend some of the dynamics of marginalization that she experienced, I needed to listen carefully to understand their particularity in her context.

I want to be clear that, although my life experiences provided an entry point to the world of this Brazilian woman, they did not provide a lens to view it. To see her reality through my lens would be another form of imperialism. What my insight allowed me to do was to listen more openly to her story so that I could more fully understand her reality. While my middle-class morality felt shaken, it was only by recalling my own experiences of oppression that I could begin to stop judging the speaker and enter into her point of view. My insight did not make me wholly uncritical of what she was saying. I still had many questions about sexist objectification and exploitation in prostitution. But it helped me understand the suffering of Brazilian women a little better, as well as the boundaries and limitations that dictate what choices are available to them for survival.

I came away with a clearer view of solidarity with poor women, especially poor Brazilian women. This entailed a commitment to study the issue further and incorporate the experiences of these women more fully into the courses I would teach. But this learning would not have occurred without connection to my own experiences of discrimination, which helped me to move through an initial resistance to the speaker to a greater openness to her story. She was a teacher to me at the time I was developing myself as a teacher. In the end this created the possibility for a greater solidarity with her because I was better able to listen and understand her situation.

This experience exemplifies a relational process that can occur for teachers or learners in a situation of diversity. We are confronted with a situation of our own ignorance about an issue, which, when revealed, can create tremendous divisiveness and personal hurt for the person in the targeted group. To make a mistake through our unintentional ignorance is not just to misunderstand, but to unwittingly cause hurt, and this foments a deeper resentment from the person who is a member of the targeted group. The unfortunate logic of oppression revolves around the fact that members of the dominant culture often cannot see the ways in which they discriminate. There is a great deal at stake in the mistakes we make as teachers and learners in multicultural settings. In fact, this is precisely the reason why the conflicts can become so great in this type of teaching—the stakes are high.

Multicultural teaching demands the formation of the teacher as a professional who forms herself spiritually as a person who is able to relate openly to her students in their totality as human beings. A student comes into a learning situation as more than just a head in which knowledge is to be deposited.[2] The student comes to learning as a whole person with intellect, affect, and physicality—all of which are formed in a social context of community. The spirituality of multicultural teaching, then, demands a formation of self with both deep self-knowledge and other-knowledge for the task of educating. It demands a keen awareness of the differences evident in the interactions between persons from different social locations. It demands an awareness of one's own participation in that network of social relations and a nuanced understanding of its dynamics.

The spirituality of multicultural teaching encompasses a deep and abiding concern for understanding identity groups in their social location of difference and teaching in a manner that honors that difference. It is a vocational commitment to teach what must be taught in a manner that makes it accessible[3] to all persons, so that the power of knowledge can be for all groups in society and not just members of the dominant culture. This is the change of understanding that multicultural pedagogy demands. A change of instructional techniques is only useful as they integrate with a holistic understanding of persons in social context.

This spiritual stance holds many implications for teachers. It insists that learning involves head, heart, and life experience. It requires that teachers understand pedagogical process as integrating several types of content in learning: academic content knowledge (from subject disciplines), social location content knowledge (from an understanding of the reality of difference in an unjust society), and experiential content knowledge (from the student's wisdom of life experience). The spiritual stance of multicultural teaching resists learning processes that ignore sociocultural differences and embraces learning processes that take them into account.

This spiritual stance also implies that a teacher understands the concept of a social analysis and knows how to use this analysis in creating effective learning. A social analysis involves analyzing a person or a group in their social context. Joe Holland and Peter Henriot define social analysis as "the effort to obtain a more complete picture of a social situation by exploring its historical and structural relationships."[4] A social analysis seeks to understand the issues of concern in a community, both historically and presently, as well as the policies that address these concerns. It seeks to understand the broader political, economic, and social structures that these policies address. All of these factors affect the life experience of a learner, and he or she brings that experience into a learning context. The spiritual stance of multicultural teaching brings this awareness into teaching design.

This spiritual stance has much in common with the perspectives of critical educational theory.[5] Although not explicitly the subject matter of this work,[6] critical educational theory engages an ideological perspective that also seeks to understand learners in their sociocultural context and to teach in ways that are appropriate to that reality. While critical educational theory focuses on ideological worldview, issues of social power, and culture, the spiritual stance of multicultural teaching attempts to integrate both intellectual and affective standpoints as well as theological points of view.

Thus, effective multicultural pedagogy demands grounding in a political awareness of persons in their social difference and in their personal experience. Teachers in a diverse context must comprehend on a rational level the reality of social structural difference, and they must comprehend on an affective level the experiences that make each student unique. Practically speaking, this means learning the ways in which poverty, racial discrimination, homophobia, handicapping conditions, or gender discrimination affect particular groups in their lived reality, and then understanding how these obstacles persist and/ or have been resisted and overcome. Individuals from marginalized groups are more than the social structural obstacles that they experience; at the same time each individual struggles with realities that members of the dominant culture do not.

Multicultural teaching demands that teachers bring a way of being in the profession that is integrated on the level of both head and heart. It demands an ability to use good judgment about interpersonal relationships in the contexts of complicated social relations. Multicultural teaching is so demanding precisely because it requires teachers to act with wisdom that takes a teaching lifetime to develop.

Perceptive Attentiveness and Multicultural Teaching

A spirituality of multicultural teaching seeks to create a process of living in the world and reflecting on one's pedagogical practice that allows teachers to become integrated persons who bring that integration to their vision of their work. A spirituality of multicultural teaching develops teachers who see the world compassionately and act in ways that concretely empower all students of the diverse context to learn.

The spirituality that develops a critical mind and a discerning heart grows from a spiritual stance that embraces perceptiveness and attentiveness. In this way the spirituality roots itself in a cognitive and affective awareness of circumstances, relationships, and emotions. Perceptiveness and attentiveness focus on both others and ourselves. It is impossible to perceive others and be attentive to them if we are unable to perceive and be attentive to ourselves. We know one another in the mutual dynamic of self and other.

To perceive means to become aware of something directly through the senses, especially sight or hearing. To perceive means to understand or apprehend. Perceptive teachers hold the ability to keenly discern and sensitively understand themselves and learners in all of their possibilities and limitations. Perceptive teachers in diverse learning environments focus especially on an awareness of the culture and social context of the learners and themselves and the relation between these different cultures. Understanding culture encompasses apprehending the customs, ideas, behaviors, worldviews, and values of various groups. Understanding social context encompasses apprehending social, political, and economic structures and power relations between groups within those structures. Thus, perceptive teachers in diverse contexts comprehend learners and themselves as individuals who exist in social relationships of culture and context.

Attentiveness involves connecting one's heart empathetically to the real experiences of people living in an unjust social system. Theologically, attentiveness involves what Thich Nhat Hanh refers to as "mindfulness," that is, "keeping one's consciousness alive in the present reality."[7] Attentiveness as mindfulness allows us to access compassion as a resource to understand the experiences of struggle that we and other human beings face.

Perceptive attentiveness can form critical minds and discerning hearts, which are fundamental groundings of multicultural teaching. Why would we want to approach our teaching in this way? The answer to that question depends on the moral values teachers attach to their work. Perceptive attentiveness anchors itself to three values that form its motivation: self-knowledge in community, solidarity, and compassion. These three values motivate teachers to engage in the hard work that the process of perceptive attentiveness engages.

A central truth that we have come to see in our global, interdependent world is that we cannot know the world, nor exist as whole persons in it, without understanding its pluralism. We do not have the option of ignoring the diversity around us. If we choose to ignore it, we are lessened as human beings. We learn about who we are in the process of learning about others. Thus, self-knowledge in community is a fundamental motivation for perceptive attentiveness.

Solidarity, understood as accountability to the just demands of a marginalized group, roots perceptive attentiveness firmly in the world and in the interactions of social power and group interests. This may be unpalatable for those who believe that spirituality has nothing to do with the problems of the world. But this misguided notion of spirituality prevents religion from being a strong advocate for justice in human relations. At the center of a diverse society stands the reality of privilege for some groups and the lack of it for others. The work of justice, and the solidarity that is part of that task, seeks to create equitable relationships between these diverse groups. As a moral demand to create right relationships, solidarity must be a fundamental concern for teaching in multicultural contexts and a primary value that grounds perceptive attentiveness.[8]

Advocacy divorced from the human emotion of empathy causes people and their concerns to become secondary to the political interests or point of view that a group represents. No teacher wants to knowingly be caught in that ideological trap. This is why compassion is a value that motivates a stance of perceptive attentiveness. Compassion contains both a deep feeling and understanding for the suffering of another and the desire to alleviate it. Compassion grounds itself in relationship to others, and is a way of life oriented toward the work of justice in the world.[9]

A critical mind and a discerning heart formed by a process of perceptive attentiveness holds an undercurrent of the values of self in community, solidarity, and compassion. They are the moral assumptions on which a spirituality of multicultural teaching can be built.

Elements of Perceptive Attentiveness

The spiritual stance of perceptive attentiveness grounds a spirituality of multicultural pedagogy. This stance has many elements that can shape our approach to teaching.

First, perceptive attentiveness demands a conversion of heart and mind. It understands that creation of a just world demands from persons a genuine turning away *(metanoia)* from fear and misunderstanding of others toward acceptance and understanding. This happens on an intellectual level at which we cognitively understand the justice issues involved and become advocates for those who are disempowered. It must also happen on an emotional level in which we accept others in Christian love. With this unity of converted mind and heart we act justly, not only because it is the right thing to do but also because it is what love demands.

This means concretely that we work as teachers to remove any fear and ignorance about our students, conscious or unconscious, that we bring into a diverse teaching context. We seek an authentic conversion that helps us to see our students truly as individuals in community, but who also, as members of specific identity groups, endure particular obstacles or experience particular privileges. We focus our teaching practices and content choices in ways that bear in mind the reality that each student brings into the learning context.

Second, perceptive attentiveness requires a politically active stance. This indicates that the work of compassion, solidarity, and self-knowledge in community concerns itself with power in the world and how it is used against some people and for others. This is the world of politics, community empowerment, and government. Perceptive attentiveness uses social analysis to gain a structural knowledge of the conditions faced by socially discriminated-against groups and seeks to strategize in the world ways to combat structural inequities through educational empowerment.

Concretely, this means that we must bring a social analysis to our understanding of our students, the content we present, and our instructional strategies. We work in multicultural teaching contexts to create a situation of educational equity in which all of the groups represented in our class can feel empowered[10] to learn in the best way that they can. At times this might mean, for example, challenging existing power structures of administration. At other times it might mean challenging the established canon of a discipline.

Third, the just transformation of an injustice against a structurally discriminated group represents the goal of perceptive attentiveness as a spiritual stance. This implies that it is also an ethical stance that seeks effective action against structural discrimination, rather than only denouncing the injustice. Acting from the perspective of perceptive attentiveness means that those with power work in solidarity with those to whom power is denied. Solidarity can only occur through a commitment that involves willingness to continually listen to and learn from others and examining and taking responsibility for the privileges received in a hegemonic society at the expense of another group.

Concretely, this means that we do not hide behind the supposed neutrality of ideas or content. We understand that all teaching involves political activity. Every decision a teacher makes about what to leave in or out is a political act. We understand the social analysis of the context in which we find ourselves. We understand that we have a significant amount of structural power over our students, and so we are responsible for using that power for equity among groups.

Perceptive Attentiveness and Critical Minds and Discerning Hearts

The spiritual stance of perceptive attentiveness grounds the development of a critical mind and a discerning heart, which is the essence of the spirituality of multicultural pedagogy. In multicultural teaching contexts, teachers must bring both an understanding of the dynamics of social hegemonies and an understanding of individual persons in their own giftedness and limitations. A stance of perceptive attentiveness that embraces self-knowledge in community, solidarity, and compassion helps form the self-awareness, empathetic sensitivity, political consciousness, and social consciousness necessary for teaching in racial, cultural, gender, and class diversity.

A critical mind understands that all persons in society live in relationship with one another as members of social groups that are either dominant or subordinate, or some measure of both, in an inequitable social order. A critical mind sees the social analysis of a teaching context and incorporates that knowledge into pedagogical practice and interaction with individual learners. Rigorous analysis places the learners, teacher, and learning environment in their social context and sees individual actions in that larger framework.

A discerning heart understands that learners are more than their social context. Each person is a self, formed in community, who has the freedom to make choices for his or her life. A discerning heart sees the person as both formed in community and social context and as a unique individual. But a discerning heart also understands that social justice is an important factor in respecting the uniqueness of each person. In fact, persons thrive best in their uniqueness when conditions of social injustice and inequity are eliminated. Thus, a discerning heart does not fear an activist stance that seeks to right the wrongs of an unjust society.

The ability to think critically is an important component of perceptive attentiveness for the development of critical minds and discerning hearts. Stephen Brookfield provides a helpful way of looking at critical thinking for teaching.[11] He articulates four central components of critical thinking: identifying and challenging assumptions; understanding the importance of context in our practices, structures, and actions; imagining and exploring alternatives; and developing a "reflective skepticism."[12] Each one provides an avenue of reflection for teachers to examine their teaching practice.

Most teachers spend endless hours in the classroom helping students identify and challenge assumptions the students hold about the content they are learning. Critical thinking for teachers must include subjecting ourselves to the same scrutiny. We need to identify and challenge the assumptions that we bring to the instruction we design, the content we teach, and the students with whom we interact. A key factor involves examining the contradictions between what we think is true with what is true in experience. Whose point of view predominates in the way we have presented our material? Whose point of view is left out? Do we make space for dissenting perspectives both in the content and from the students themselves? What do we assume about the students? Do we assume that they have no experience with the material we are teaching? Do we have cultural assumptions? What biases do we bring to the class context? Because our assumptions are often hidden to us, we must be intentional about identifying them and subjecting them to rigorous examination.

For example, Brookfield examines an uncritical use of the instructional technique of placing students in a circle for class discussion. He notes that for some students and in certain contexts this may be experienced as invasive, coercive, and pressuring. Critiquing his own educational practice and assumptions, he asserts,

> The circle can be experienced as a mechanism for mandated disclosure, just as much as it can be a chance for people to speak in an authentic voice…I continue to use the circle in my own practice. But critical reflection makes me aware of the circle's oppressive potential and reminds me that I must continually research how it is experienced by students.[13]

When we begin to see how unconscious and influential our assumptions can be, we become more alert to the ways that context influences our perspective of the world. However, a danger can develop for teachers if we allow this awareness of perspective to blind us to the evolving nature of social context. We cannot limit learners according to what we perceive to be defining contextual characteristics. We cannot allow contextual awareness to be another box that we fit learners into that prevents us from seeing clearly who the learners are and what they need. Also, we need to examine ourselves in our social context, integrating that analysis with our understanding of the learners in their social context.

In reflecting on an incident with a white male student of German heritage, Asian American scholar Patricia Sakurai notes that understanding the context of the classroom must include examining the dynamics of the discussions and the interactions of people, including herself. She comments, "For all my abilities to link content and context with the texts I read, I failed to do the same when it came to the content and context of the learning situation in which I myself was involved."[14] She goes on to critique her teaching practice, understanding her own social location as a significant factor in class dynamics and seeking to examine the ways in which she could be essentializing herself or her students in class.

Examining and exploring alternatives provides energy in the teaching process. However, learning to teach in a way that attends to cultural diversity can force us as teachers to consider alternatives that might be challenging, uncomfortable, or even threatening. These alternatives might reconfigure ways that we understand subject matter or even an academic discipline itself. Denise Dombkowski Hopkins, Sharon H. Ringe, and Frederick C. Tiffany offer an interesting critique of the field of biblical studies as it confronts the Bible in global context. They speak of the "endurance of critical consensus" in which traditional ways of studying biblical texts remain the dominant paradigm. Even when diverse voices are acknowledged, a "muffling" of those voices occurs in two ways: first, through assigning these texts as sidelines and extras to the traditional critical task, which remains Eurocentric and male; and second, through neutralizing the particularity of the cultural voices by insisting they be spoken only in a narrowly defined notion of academic discourse.[15] If teachers are to function effectively in multicultural classrooms, we must allow diverse voices to challenge our basic understanding of how subject matter is to be considered.

Critical thinking that leads to what Brookfield calls "reflective skepticism" demands a willingness to challenge our own fixed and deep-rooted, perhaps even sacred, notions of what we know about learners, subject matter, and pedagogical practices. In this sense the reflective skepticism of critical thinking demands a rigorous and courageous scrutiny of our worldviews.

The capacity for having a critical mind and a discerning heart is not an infused gift that we either have or do not have. While it is true that we are born with differing gifts for empathy or analysis, we can learn ways to develop a critical mind and a discerning heart through intellectual and spiritual discipline that combines both analytic and soul learning. The next chapters articulate listening and understanding, seeing clearly, and acting differently as ways to begin this vital learning.

Reflection on Teaching Practice

We build our integrity through the daily activity of teaching. Each decision we make, each interaction with learners, builds our teaching character. If our decisions are authoritarian, coercive, or mean-spirited, then the teaching character that we develop will be likewise. Alternately, if our decisions are fair, learner-centered, and empowering, then we develop a teaching character of genuine moral grounding. In many ways, the spiritual stance of perceptive attentiveness seeks to develop character that creates coherence between what we want our teaching to be and what, in fact, our practice is.

Our teaching practices are often the unexamined elements of what we actually teach. In teaching content, we cannot deny that we are the messengers of that content. We also teach a great deal through our teaching practices. Teaching theologies of liberation with practices that are transmissive or indoctrinating gives learners a mixed message. Teaching about social hegemonies with a hegemonic pedagogical practice contradicts the intended learning. The demands of teaching rarely allow us time and space to examine the messages our teaching practices give.

In a multicultural context we need to form a teaching character grounded in *humility*. One given in any teaching context is that the teacher will never know all that there is to know about a subject. However, when we combine that fact with the plurality of viewpoints existing in a diverse teaching setting, then we increase the amount of information that a teacher may not know. When we add to that reality the explosion of scholarship that exists in most fields, the complexity of intercultural communication, and the knowledge a teacher needs to communicate across the boundaries of that difference, it seems daunting and intimidating to even attempt to teach. It can be quite overwhelming to think about what a teacher needs to know to teach effectively! Humility about what is possible in that complicated context—and what we are capable of, given our own limitations—helps us face the enormity of the task.

This does not mean that we reject our responsibility to be knowledgeable in our subject area and pedagogical practice. It does mean that teaching in a multicultural context demands that we reject any notion that adult learners bring no knowledge or experience from their lives that might be relevant for learning. Teaching in a diverse context requires the humility to realize that an aspect of our job is to facilitate the knowledge already present among the learners and that we perhaps do not have. We are both teachers and learners in any teaching context, but this is especially true in multicultural teaching contexts. Whether we are members of the dominant culture in that learning environment or a member of a minority culture, we use our power to help facilitate the plurality of viewpoints that exist on any topic. Our own voice should never be the only voice in the room that we hear!

1. What do we notice most about the students we teach? How does this knowledge affect or not affect the way that we teach them?
2. Draw an image or play music that speaks to you of perceptiveness and attentiveness. What does the image or music tell you about yourself as a teacher? In what ways can you incorporate this awareness into your pedagogical practice?
3. What teaching practice do you use most commonly in your class? What message does it send to the students about the subject matter you are teaching? Is it the message that you want to send?
4. Consider your subject matter. What is "awesome" about it? What aspect of that subject matter do you find the most humbling in terms of your ability to understand it fully?

2

Listening and Understanding

It was my first trip to Africa. Faculty representatives from seminaries in Africa and the United States had assembled in Morija, Lesotho, for an international, ecumenical meeting on global theological education.[1] As I saw the group of twenty assemble, I realized that there was a very good possibility that I was the only female member of this consultation. The group was a mixture of African, African American, and European American men. Later in the weeklong consultation, an African female colleague from the National Teacher Training College in Maseru came for a few days to join the gathering, but for a significant portion of the time I was the only woman present. This was unusual for me in theological education circles in the United States. Although as a woman faculty member I was often in the numerical minority in theological gatherings, and had experiences of sexism and discrimination, rarely had I been the only female in a professional gathering. Furthermore, I was also the only Roman Catholic member in the predominantly Protestant group.

One particular experience (of the many interesting events of that trip) stands out as significant to the subject of this chapter.

At the end of one of the days, our group took a short trip to visit the church of one of our members in the nearby village of Matieng, which is also the home of the royal family of Lesotho. We experienced wonderful hospitality both at the local church and in the local village. Later, the group was escorted around the back of the home of the royal family in order to meet the king's uncle. At this point, the two of us who were women were separated from the group and not permitted to participate in this conversation. There was great confusion among the men as to what to do in this circumstance. Some wanted to stay with us; some did not want to proceed; and some were unaware that it had happened because they were farther ahead of the main group. My female colleague and I told them to go without us, wishing not to be the center of a controversy with a member of the royal family. (We found out later that one of the African men asked the member of the royal family if he would permit us to join the conversation. This did not happen, though.)

When we returned to the conference center in Morija and began to discuss the experience, I was the only woman at the table because my female colleague had returned to Maseru for the evening to be with her family. The meeting facilitator summed up the conversation well in his report:

> We began by commenting on the initial hospitality of the villagers, who with little extra food, offered us generous and significant portions. We remarked on how hospitality in Africa has been incorporated into the theology and how African hospitality has survived in the African American community in the United States. However, though all of us enjoyed the initial and more humble hospitality, all of us did not enjoy hospitality when we were separated. Women experienced something altogether different. We wanted to respect local culture but felt awkward having been together as a group until this moment. Thus we experienced hospitality, exclusion and separation all at the same time.[2]

Indeed, the experience was confusing, contentious, and complicated for all involved. Both the Americans and Africans wanted to respect the local custom because we were guests in that area. However, there were significant issues that many, both African and American, had with this custom. Some of the Africans expressed concern about American cultural imperialism, represented in feminist concerns interfering with their tribal customs. Other Africans challenged their colleagues on the issue of sexism. European Americans challenged African colleagues about the lack of women in theological education in Africa. The African American men stated that they felt trapped in the middle between gender and race issues, between their own feminist inclinations and their African male colleagues.

In this complicated mix I sat at the table as the only one present in the conversation who had experienced exclusion. It struck me that, for the most part, many of the men were talking about the incident and my exclusion as if I were not present! I was the one who had experienced the exclusion, yet few seemed aware of my presence. It was difficult for me to listen to some of the more problematic statements about women and equality that were part of the conversation. It was clear that my point of view, and that of my female colleague, were largely absent in the discussion. When I spoke, I challenged them about this absence. I also challenged them to think about why they were drawing separate moral categories for the separation and exclusion of women and the separation and exclusion of races. How would the situation have been different, I asked them, if the custom was that all of the darker-skinned persons were to be excluded?

Sitting at that table, I felt angry and isolated to a degree that I had not before in a professional context. While I appreciated that many of the men were taking responsibility to bring the issue to the forefront, rather than leaving it up to me, I resented being left out of the discussion as if I were incidental to the circumstance. I also resented that in this discussion the point of view was still largely male, yet I would have hated being put on the spot to express "the woman's point of view." Mainly, I wanted to be somewhere else than in this discussion! The conflict was making me quite tense; I felt this odd juxtaposition of being both invisible and exposed. Yet it was a battle that had to be endured because larger issues were at stake that had to do with fairness.

Suddenly, I thought, "This is what it must be like for people of color in a white-dominant setting." It was an explosive insight that grounded me in that discussion and for much of the rest of the consultation. I began to see my experience in a larger context of dominant group and minority group dynamics. I am not saying that I now understood what people of color feel in white-dominated settings, but rather my insight gave me new ears to listen and an opened mind for understanding how experiences of racial identity isolation in a dominant group context might feel. It gave me a greater sense of empathy for the experiences of another group that exists in a different social location from me.

As I later reflected on this insight, I recalled an experience I had in the classroom some years ago that had to do with an issue of racial isolation. As a young graduate student I was teaching a seminary course on pedagogical practices. In the first session, as we went over the syllabus, an African American man, who was the only person of color in the class, challenged me, saying, "There are no authors from communities of color in this syllabus." It was not hostile, but it was assertive and painfully accurate. Not only did I feel inadequate as a teacher, I also was struggling against the type of "white guilt" feelings that occur when you are "caught in the act" of your unconscious racism. (Such feelings help no one in that circumstance. I have long ago learned that those feelings must be dealt with on your own time, and not with the expectation that the person of color will absolve you from your guilt.) He was absolutely correct. The readings were not diverse and said nothing about his educational experiences. I agreed with him and said that I would rectify the problem for next week's class. As I went about "doing my homework" properly, I realized the poverty of that previous syllabus.

Looking back from the perspective of my experience of isolation in Africa, I have some sense of what this man might have experienced with my syllabus. Very likely, he had experienced the feeling of exclusion in his classroom environment one too many times and had decided to challenge professors on their conscious or unconscious exclusions. While he was clearly irritated at having to bring it up, he did not necessarily want to be the center of attention and the spokesperson for the issue. He probably wished that he did not have to deal with it at all, but a larger issue was at stake here. He was also very likely irritated that he had to teach this white woman about her unconscious racism. Thankfully, I knew enough about the educational system and its dynamics of racism, that as soon as he challenged me I knew exactly what the problem was. He did not have to explain it further.

Through my own experience of exclusion and isolation at that international meeting, I now feel, years later, that I have a better grasp of the dynamics of that particular teaching situation. I have a better experiential awareness of the feelings of isolation and anger my student very likely had. This knowledge comes with me into all my teaching contexts as I try to listen to my students and understand the dynamics of identity isolation.

This chapter reflects on the skills of listening and understanding, two of the most important competencies that any teacher must have. Because they are such an integrative process, they are purposely paired. Listening demands attentiveness to another, an active participation in what that person is revealing. But the goal of listening is not only hearing, but to understand. We listen so that we may know more fully and completely. We cannot understand if we do not listen. At the same time, increased understanding allows us to listen with greater sensitivity and comprehension. When we listen deeply, we can begin to comprehend another. When we can comprehend another more fully, we can begin to listen with more sophistication, more capable of hearing the nuances of human communication.

Without these skills we cannot comprehend who we are, let alone who our students are as persons or what they need in order to learn. Self-knowledge is a primary prerequisite for being able to understand others. With self-knowledge comes perspective, which allows us to see others in context. Without knowledge of who we are in our own identity, we run the danger of projecting our own unresolved or unwanted issues onto others. In this scenario, we impose on our students what we think they need to know, rather than attending to what they tell us they need to know.

Listening and understanding are much easier to do in theory than to live out in reality. Often we think that we are really listening, only to discover that we have completely missed what was being communicated to us. It is difficult enough to do well in a monocultural teaching context. In a multicultural teaching context the task becomes increasingly more difficult and complex.

The listening and understanding that are the subject of this chapter have to do with an attentiveness to marginalization experiences, both in ourselves and in others, that might be part of the teaching dynamics in diverse settings. This attentiveness incorporates the ways in which we relate to ourselves and to others. But, most importantly, it incorporates the ways in which we relate to the world as a community of persons who are in relationship to one another through social institutions. Specifically, the discipline of listening and understanding involves attentiveness to the following concerns:

- seeking to understand our own experiences of marginalization, or lack of it, in relation to the experiences of others
- trying to understand the marginalization experiences of others empathetically
- seeing our own and others' experiences of marginalization, in perspective from the context of social structural power,

and the privilege of some groups over other groups in a hegemonic society

The discipline of listening and understanding depends on our comprehension of the interaction between the marginalization that a person experiences and the reality of that person as a member of a social grouping within the power relations of an unequal society. Teaching in diverse contexts depends on attentiveness to these issues because they anchor our teaching practice in a combination of concrete analysis of social relationships and affective care for the well-being of others.

One caveat cannot be restated strongly enough: *Empathy for another's experience cannot be an excuse to appropriate that experience and make it our own.* We cannot take over an issue that rightly belongs in another's experience and make it about us. As I stated in the critical incident in the previous chapter, our ability to relate to another's experience does not give us a lens through which to view it. However, what it can do is give us a way to begin to listen and understand another's experience more faithfully.

Also, it is important to note that attentive awareness of marginalization experiences in others and ourselves does not necessarily occur sequentially as I have listed them above. Insight can come in any way that God provides it. Yet these three perspectives must interplay with one another in some way for the discipline of listening and understanding to be fully embodied. The combination of self, other, and social context is imperative for listening clearly and understanding fully.

Finally, it is important to remember that human nature moves through personal change and greater awareness slowly, with one step forward and two steps back. Attentiveness to listening and understanding often happens in experiences of conflict, anger, and miscommunication. Those aspects, while not ignored in this chapter, will be discussed more fully in the following chapter.

Attentive Awareness in Interaction

It may seem odd to engage our own experiences of marginalization and exclusion when trying to understand how to relate to others. It seems selfish and self-absorbed. Yet it is, at times, a fundamental starting point. Knowing our own experience of marginalization and its pain makes sense of the obstacles that we have faced, resisted, and overcome or are, at least, working to overcome. In comprehending our own marginalization, we can come to know in our very being what it feels like to experience it, and thus, that comprehension can begin to make us more empathetic with the pain others experience because of their marginalization.

In turning away from our marginalization experiences, we can begin to project that pain onto others. This is tremendously dangerous for anyone in a helping profession, and teachers are not exempt from this. When teaching (or ministering) becomes more about our needs and ignores the needs of learners, then we are in serious trouble, both practically and ethically.

There is a danger, though, in becoming stuck in our own experiences of marginalization. This is the danger of narcissism—a situation in which we are so stuck in our own problems that we are unable to see beyond them. They grip and control us. We feel helpless to overcome these feelings. In this instance it should be a sign to us that we are not in an emotional position to teach, especially in a context of diversity in which we could do great harm.

Understanding our own experiences of the hurt suffered from discrimination can help us to be in greater solidarity with the pain of others. Cherríe Moraga believes that solidarity can only occur when we understand the sources of our oppression: "Without an emotional, heartfelt grappling with the sources of our own oppression, without naming the enemy within ourselves and outside of us, no authentic, non-hierarchical connection among oppressed groups can take place."[3] Without this awareness of our own woundedness, our action for solidarity could become either patronizing or dislocated from the reality of human interconnectedness: When one suffers, we all suffer; no one is free unless all of us are free. Also, without this awareness we could naively assume that we are not affected by the structures of domination that oppress another group.

As a white person, for example, if I wish to be in solidarity with people of color against the oppression of racism, I must understand both the concrete ramifications of racist discrimination on people of color, as well as my own privileged exemption from those issues. No one is completely exempt from the effects of racism. I must be aware of how the privileges I receive in a white racist structure diminish my own humanness because those privileges are received at the cost of another's dehumanization.

Moraga provides a useful story that exemplifies how the work of understanding our own experiences of oppression is essential in our coming to understand another person's experience of oppression. She states that the point of departure lies in an awareness of the particular oppression(s) that affects us. But, she cautions, to remain stuck in an awareness of our own suffering, without a movement to use it to understand the suffering of others, "will only isolate us in our own oppression—will only insulate, rather than radicalize us."[4] She illustrates this point with a story about a friend.

> A gay male friend of mine once confided to me that he continued to feel that, on some level, I didn't trust him because he was male...He wanted to understand the source of my distrust. I responded, "You're not a woman. Be a woman for a day. Imagine being a woman." He confessed that the thought terrified him because, to him, being a woman meant being raped by men. He felt raped by men; he wanted to forget what that meant. What grew from that discussion was the realization that in order for him to create an authentic

alliance with me, he must deal with the primary source of his own sense of oppression. He must first, emotionally come to terms with what it feels like to be a victim. If he—or anyone—were to truly do this, it would be impossible to discount the oppression of others, except by again forgetting how we have been hurt.[5]

Many times our inability to work through our own issues of pain from social oppression becomes a barrier to compassionate action. Our action can turn into an unconscious attempt to resolve our suffering at the expense of the other with whom we are supposedly in solidarity. This often leads to hurting the other when our intention is to help. Merle Woo vividly describes this experience of working with women who have not dealt with their own pain, stating, "I get so tired of being the instant resource for information on Asian American women. Being the token representative, going from class to class, group to group, bleeding for white women so they can have an easy answer."[6] The danger of an inability to deal with our own pain is the risk that we will let those with whom we want to be in solidarity "bleed" for us, rather than doing our own work to resolve the pain.

Being attentive to our own marginalization is never something that we discover in isolation. We understand our suffering better when we understand others' suffering and when we work to be in solidarity with them. We are relational beings who come to greater personal awareness in our attempts to interact with others in the world. For example, Minnie Bruce Pratt's coming out as a lesbian heightened her awareness of racism and anti-Semitism. She writes,

> When…I groped toward an understanding of injustice done to others, injustice done outside my narrow circle of being, and to folks not like me, I began to grasp, through my own experience, something of what that

injustice might be, began to feel the extent of pain, anger, desire for change."[7]

Her experience of heterosexual privilege pushed her into an awareness of the extent of structural discrimination and how insulated she had previously been from its existence: "The shell of my privilege was broken, the shell that had given me a shape in the world, held me apart from the world, protected me from the world. I was astonished at the pain; the extent of my surprise revealed to me the degree of my protection."[8] Thus, through the loss of privilege, she became sensitized to discrimination against others, as well as learning more about her own marginalization.

This example can be spun out further. For example, I might be acutely aware of the discrimination experienced in a heterosexist society as a lesbian woman. But understanding the oppression of poor persons or physically challenged persons can help in an understanding of my personal experience of discrimination. Although different marginalized groups experience discrimination in ways particular to them, the experience of facing systemic oppression has at least one common element: Structural discrimination imposes barriers and obstacles to getting basic needs met for human survival. As a white lesbian woman I cannot know totally what it is like to experience racism, but I can begin to understand the nature of the structures of racist oppression by connecting to my own experience of being discriminated against as a homosexual. In this way, my understanding of my particular marginalization is heightened as well as my understanding of the marginalization of others, which in the end can increase my ability to be in solidarity.

This dynamic interaction cannot be produced or conjured. To do so would be to create a political correctness or a coercion of thinking. All we can do in the classroom is to offer readings and design pedagogical processes that will create the best possible condition for the insight experiences to occur naturally, in their own time. Like any insight, self-knowledge and knowledge of others arise out of their own process and cannot be predicted or programmed.

Before my doctoral program, I worked in a social justice education program at a Jesuit university. I remember distinctly a young white, working-class man I worked with who felt the need to fight with me on every issue that involved the church and society's response to persons living in poverty. In his mind, he had pulled himself up out of poverty and made his way to college; therefore, everyone should be able to do so. In our conversations and interactions, I knew I would be limited in what I would be able to accomplish in terms of helping him to see those issues more broadly and critically. What I could do was help him to see the ways in which he faced major obstacles as a working-class man and try to help him make the connections to the obstacles others face. The more I could help him to see the reality of social structural discrimination connected to his own life and to the lives of others, the more he could begin to listen more clearly to others and understand their experience. He never did completely see a way to comprehend all of those factors. I had to respect where he was in his thinking process and give him space to find his own answers. Insights come in their own time, or maybe not at all. As teachers we need to accept that reality.

With greater ability to listen and understand, and knowledge of social power and how it is used for or against persons, teachers can learn to understand the experiences of persons who are from a different social location. We can begin to listen more carefully and understand more fully if we have some sense what it means to experience marginalization— perhaps not this particular type of marginalization, but one that has *similar dynamics* in terms of social structural discrimination. This is a key point. Our empathy is limited until we begin to see another person's marginalization in the context of the social structural obstacles that are in place for that person. When we can do this, we heighten our ability to act in solidarity with others, with a sense of genuine compassion.

Without social structural analysis, our perspective is limited only to the personal and interpersonal. Prejudice and discrimination are more than just a few misguided men who hate women, or a few white bigots who hate people of color. Rather, prejudice and discrimination include inequities incorporated into the social systems of a society. Thus, sexism is both a personal action that is discriminatory and a worldview that establishes the dominance of men over women in politics, healthcare, and economics. Racism is both a personal prejudicial action and a worldview of white supremacy that is woven into cultural, economic, and political systems. Social analysis helps us to see our interaction with both diversity and difference in perspective.

Social analysis can be a powerful way to learn to listen and to understand. Comprehending the contradictions between our experiences and the experiences of others can be a powerful tool for learning compassion. I once worked with a student in field education who had a powerful experience, from his work in a social service agency, of understanding the marginalization of others, the social structures that caused this discrimination, and his advantages in relation to those structures. This young man was from wealth and privilege. He often felt threatened in the diverse setting of Union by the challenges he received from students to see the ways in which he profited from a social system designed to benefit him. This summer field practicum (between his second and third year of seminary) was his first encounter interacting with persons who experience poverty and structural discrimination. I remember speaking with him when he returned from his summer experience. He was tremendously upset and overwhelmed at what he had seen and the stories that he had heard from the people who were his clients. He told me, "I never knew that the world was so unjust for so many people—and not for me." This was profound learning for him that books could not have provided in the same way. The experiential learning about social structural discrimination, seared into him, helped him to comprehend the pain of others more clearly and to see his own privilege. His compassion was strengthened from realizing the contradictions between his life and the lives of others in a very different social location.

Learning to Listen and Understand

One way that we can learn to listen and to understand is to develop our ability to be in touch with our own woundedness. This is the emotional aspect of marginalization. When we are attentive to the ways in which social discrimination has marginalized us, and the ways in which it wounds us, we can access our compassion much more freely and with greater depth of feeling. With greater compassion, we can commit to greater solidarity with those who are disempowered in the social system.

In *Common Fire: Leading Lives of Commitment in a Complex World,* the authors provide a helpful example in which attentiveness to our woundedness has the potential to lead to compassion and solidarity.[9] They highlight the story of Luisandra Hernandez, a physician who is a nationally recognized leader in public health issues. She lived for much of her early life with a heart condition that could have been corrected had her family had the money for the needed surgery. Her confrontation with the gap in health care access between rich and poor led her to her work for justice in medical access through public health and education.

When we do not know our own woundedness, we can do unconscious damage because we do not comprehend how we are taking our pain out on others. As John Haughey writes,

> [T]o the extent that we do not know ourselves, we are continually making victims or inciting tensions that require others to be compassionate to those we have hurt, however unconsciously. By greater self-knowledge

we can reduce or eliminate the social tension, hostility, or violence we ourselves are causing.[10]

Resisting the honest appraisal of our own woundedness can cause harm to others no matter whether we are members of the dominant group or the targeted group. Because of the social power of each group, the harm is different, but harmful nonetheless.

A second way we can learn to listen and to understand is to make every attempt to *educate ourselves* about social groups that we do not know. This education primarily consists of hearing the stories of those who have different experiences than we have. We can hear these stories from participating in diverse educational contexts and by reading their stories as they have told them. The more that we know about a group's history, their experiences with the social systems of society, and their access or lack of access to social power, the more we can interact in diverse contexts as colleagues and allies.

Lacking knowledge of the diverse groups in society and in our classrooms can lead to serious cultural damage from the educational process. For example, Jace Weaver articulates the effect on Native American religious education as a result of teachers and missionaries not educating themselves about the Native communities. He writes,

> When the indigenous peoples of the Americas have impinged at all upon the consciousness of religious educators, it has been as the subjects of missionization rather than as living beings whose culture and worldview have something important to contribute to our understanding of the Creator and the created order. Religious education given to Native Americans has reflected a monocultural imposition on a multicultural reality.[11]

As teachers we must educate ourselves as fully as we are able about the culture of the groups with whom we interact. Otherwise, we risk losing the liberatory potential of education.

A third way that we can learn to listen and to understand is to make a commitment to *create more space in our pedagogy for students to find their own voices.* When we make this commitment, we commit ourselves to "hear one another to speech."[12] In this way we create a community of listeners who can better understand one another's experiences. Many teachers believe this in theory but will often ignore it in their teaching practice. The reason is usually something to the effect that "I must cover the content!" We at times ignore the fact that there are *multiple contents* in any class situation. One content is the subject matter. Another is the content of the learning process itself—what we learn from our interactions with each other and the material. Another content is our lives—what we learn about ourselves as human beings from this learning process and subject matter. When we commit ourselves to making more space for emerging voices, we are making a commitment to the multiple contents of students' experiences and their integration in the class learning. In this way we promote a developing discerning heart, capable of hearing the stories of others more empathetically.

A fourth way we can learn to listen and to understand is to attend to the *contradictions* that we observe in our social interactions between groups of persons. Contradictions help us to see the ways in which the rhetoric of a society and its actions are not coherent. They can be seen by trying to understand the societal divisions that exist between persons because of race, gender, sexual orientation, class, religion, disability status, and so forth. We can observe the contradictions in the experiences of different groups by asking several important questions: (1) Who makes the decisions and has the access to the most power in this context? (2) Who benefits from the decision and to what end? (3) Who bears the cost of the decision, and is it right to ask them to bear it? When we ask these critical questions, we can begin to discern the ways in which the contradictions between what a society says and what a society does plays out in the everyday lives of people.

In this way we promote a developing critical mind that comprehends the reality of difference in an inequitable society.

When we are able to listen and to understand those from different social locations than ours, we are able to change the way we see and interact with them. In fact, the colloquial expressions "I see" and "I hear you" mean to comprehend meaning. When we listen compassionately and with critical awareness of the contradictions of lived experience, we begin to understand, and so we begin to see more clearly.

Reflection on Teaching Practice

The notion of interpreting the "signs of the times" has been tumbling around in my consciousness while writing this chapter. This is a theological idea that is quite common for Vatican II Roman Catholics. The most common usage is associated with the council document "Pastoral Constitution on the Church in the Modern World *(Gaudium et Spes)*".[13] The concept might have apocalyptic connotations for some Protestant theologies, but for Catholic theology it has a very positive meaning. The signs of the times are "those events of history through which God continues to speak to us and summon us to respond for the sake of the reign of God's love and justice throughout the whole of creation."[14] It is a positive emphasis that connects the church to the world. When we interpret the signs of the times, we are discerning the Spirit of God in the world and using that revelation to transform creation into its right relation. It is way that we can learn to listen and to understand on a communal, religious level.

How can we discern the signs of the times in our teaching practice? In what ways do we perceive the Spirit of God operating in our teaching experiences? What are the ways in which we ignore it or miss it altogether? Another way to ask the questions might be this: How do we discern God's Spirit at work in multicultural educational settings? What are the ways in which we resist God's Spirit or miss it entirely?

For this reflection I would like to focus on the ways we miss signs that are before us. I do this not out of a pessimism about our teaching abilities or personal sensitivities, but because of the simple fact that it is harder to examine that which we do not see. I assume we could all use more reflection on this matter!

One of the real difficulties of multicultural teaching involves the degree to which communication is unclear in the classroom between students and students, or between students and teachers. In these instances, for example, a Native American, Asian American, or Hispanic student might question the polarized race politics of black/white and be heard as unwilling to engage the reality of racial conflict between African American and European American persons. The conflict that likely erupts from this type of miscommunication may cause us as teachers to miss the signs of God's presence in that encounter. The signs of the times in that conflict might be challenging us to understand racial dynamics in a broader perspective and to be in solidarity more widely than we have understood. When we do not pay sufficient attention to the action of God in the pedagogical process, we can miss the signs of the times in our classrooms. Caught up in the moment of conflict, we can miss the positive opportunity for growth and increased awareness that constructive conflict can engender. Rather, out of fear of the conflict, we might ignore it or remain in denial to its existence. In this instance, we ignore the signs of God's activity in the class in and through the tensions we encounter.

Sometimes we miss the signs of the times because we are not aware of the diversity that exists in our student audience. Perhaps we are aware of the visible diversity of gender, race, and ethnicity, but we are unaware of the invisible diversity that exists and is a definite influence on classroom dynamics. Students might have a disability that is not visible and that they do not disclose. Students may seek privacy on issues such as sexual orientation, substance abuse recovery, or abuse survival.

This diversity may or may not become a subject for discussion in class, but it exists in the class nonetheless. The point is that our students enter our classes as whole human beings, not just as minds alone. The unseen diversity students bring is just as much a part of the pedagogical dynamics as the visible diversity.

How do we interpret the signs of the times—how do we discern God's Spirit so as to learn to listen and understand—when there is no obvious diversity? That is, how do we discern God's Spirit at work in an educational setting that *on first look* appears monocultural? This monocultural setting could be, for example, one with a single racial, gender, or economic grouping. Rather than concerning a specific monocultural grouping, the question is really about educational settings that have a predominance of one identity grouping, and that group experience becoming predominant in class interactions.

One way to interpret the signs of the times in an apparently monocultural setting is to assume that there is something we are missing. With this *hermeneutic of suspicion,* we can critically examine what is missing in the context. Here are some questions that we should ask ourselves as teacher, when the group context is apparently monocultural and seems to only have one point of view.

- What questions are not being asked? Which groups are not asking questions? Why?
- Whose perspective is being left out? Whose perspective is dominating?
- Who, *more precisely,* is our "audience"? Do we need to reassess our comprehension of the composition of the class?
- Have we done an adequate needs assessment of the group? Have we asked the fundamental question, "Who needs what as defined by whom?"[15]
- In order to be clear about what we are missing in the classroom dynamic, what questions do we need to ask directly of the students?

Critical questioning of our teaching praxis can create a more open climate in a multicultural classroom. When we model for our students ways to be more inclusive, we are not only being effective teachers pedagogically, we are also educating the students about ways to be better citizens in a global society.

We need to ask ourselves these questions in an ostensibly diverse setting as well. In fact, the more we explore the composition of our classes, the more we will find greater diversity than originally thought. If we are teaching well, then we are creating more and more space for increasing diversity of experience and point of view. Keep this in mind as you ponder these questions:

1. In what ways do you make space in the class for students to bring their life experiences, in connection to the material, for reflection? Do some ways work better than others?
2. In what ways do you balance personal, interpersonal, and social structural perspectives in your course content?
3. What helps you to listen more carefully to your students? What specific teaching practices help you to listen to and to understand your students more accurately?
4. Is there a specific spiritual or teaching practice that helps you to be more aware of God's action in the teaching process?

3

Seeing Clearly

Several years ago a Korean pastor asked me to come to his church to speak to his congregation on the topic of homosexuality. His congregants were mostly young Korean and Korean American undergraduate and graduate students from Columbia University. He explained to me that recently there had been much discussion in the group about the issue, without the chance of speaking directly with someone who was openly homosexual. It was clear to me from his statements that there was some tension and discomfort with the issue, and he was asking me to speak so as to personalize it for some of the students. He also explained that there was a mix in the group of language facility with English, so he would translate my remarks to them and their questions to me. The teacher in me eagerly agreed to speak with this church group. The lesbian in me, however, felt an appropriate anxiety at the prospect of taking on the role of "professional lesbian" in a potentially contentious environment.

This configuration of circumstances is very common in diverse teaching contexts. Any teacher is part of an identity group that exists within specified power relations in society, yet has power and authority in that context that others do not have. The teacher, for example, might be a Hispanic woman from a working-class background, but is teaching a class that is populated by upper middle-class white high school boys. In that context she may experience all of the assumptions and prejudices that are directed at Hispanic working-class women. Yet she has an institutional control and power that the students do not. However, as a teacher from a minority group, she must deal with the contradiction of having institutional power that nonetheless exists within the unjust power relations of social prejudice. When she experiences the inevitable conscious or unconscious undermining of her authority as teacher, it creates an emotional drain that can be painful for her on a personal level.

I was aware of this dynamic as I prepared for the conversation. This was going to be an experience in which each of us would struggle to understand the other, with language differences as part of the mix. I understood no Korean and was dependent on the pastor to translate my words accurately to the group. I was putting my trust in him as a mediator of my remarks to a group with a number of "issues" with people like me. (Happily, I knew the pastor well enough to trust him.) Most of the students, as well as the pastor, identified themselves as Koreans who were in the United States for school, with only a few identifying as Korean American. I wondered what this group knew about the Italian American culture of my heritage, or whether I would be lumped into the general category of "White Westerner." I was fearful on some level about the degree of rejection I might experience as a lesbian and a woman in this Asian culture. I am sure they wondered what, if anything, I knew about Korean and Korean American culture and history, the racism and imperialism they have experienced as a people, and their cultural notions about sexuality in general and homosexuality in particular. Also, we had to bridge the gap between the Korean/Korean American Methodist and U.S. Roman Catholic religious worldviews. All in all, there was potential for disaster for them as well as for me.

One of the important preparations I do for this type of teaching situation is to prepare myself emotionally for the conscious or unconscious insults that I will inevitably experience in a context where people are struggling with their judgments about homosexuality. In fact, a teacher who willingly puts himself into this type of situation—teaching about one's own particularity (race, gender, class, disability, etc.) in the presence of those who are other to that reality—must realize that learning occurs to the degree that those prejudices are surfaced and dealt with openly. I generally prepare in two ways.

First, I center myself in prayer and biblical reading, reaffirming for myself God's love for me as I am created (Psalm 139:13–16), and understanding that nothing can sever me from the love of God (Romans 8:37–39). I also remind myself of God's protection of me in a hostile environment, giving me words to say (Luke 12:11–12), and the reality that God is always with me (Psalm 63:1–8).

Second, I center myself as a teacher. I focus on the task at hand, carefully preparing both the content and the pedagogical design. I remind myself that personalizing the painful statements will not help the students learn. I focus my attention on the fact that teaching is about the students and what they need to learn, and not primarily about my needs.

Finally, I center myself emotionally. I attend to my own needs for safety (understanding that this is a relative term in this situation), security, and affirmation. I prepare potential responses for what I anticipate will be the most difficult questions. Also, I try to arrange supports for myself for after the event, returning into a supportive environment where I am not "other" and do not have to be so defended.

For this teaching experience I made time before the event to pray and center myself, and I planned a small gathering with friends afterwards to release any possible toxicity that might build up. In preparation for the actual class, I spoke in detail with the pastor about the group composition, their questions and concerns about homosexuality that had surfaced, what they already knew about the topic, their needs for learning, and their preferences in instructional styles. I also spent a good bit of time speaking with a Korean friend about Korean culture and religion, attitudes about sexuality and homosexuality, and reactions to female professors. This friend expressed a desire to come to the class, which I accepted gratefully and with real appreciation for the support.

On the evening of the class, the pastor graciously introduced me to the group. They were bright and clearly interested in speaking with me, even though I could sense some anxiety from them. I had decided that a useful instructional strategy would be to lecture briefly about my life experience as a lesbian, coming out, and the role of religion in that process and in my life currently. From that basis we would begin the discussion.

The students politely listened to the lecture as the pastor translated it to them. I had been warned by the pastor and by my friend that I should expect very little response afterwards because they would likely be hesitant to engage the subject matter or me. In actuality, these students were the opposite of what we all expected! They immediately peppered me with questions and comments, some direct and some indirect. There was the usual amount of prejudicial statements that were difficult to hear as a lesbian, but I was able to put my personal feelings aside for the moment and allow my teacher-self to use the opportunity for important experiential learning. The spiritual centering I had done in preparation helped immensely. Overall, there was a good deal of honest dialogue in which these students were trying to understand something that was for many of them a very problematic issue.

In general, the students were engaging in two activities that are typical for this type of multicultural teaching situation. First, they were challenging me to defend my orientation and life, given the religious and cultural prescriptions that influenced them. They wanted to know how I could live a life that to them contradicted everything that they understood about morality and respectability—and be a professor at a seminary! Second, they were asking candid questions in order to challenge their lack of knowledge about a subject that confused many of them. Clearly, homosexuality was less of an issue for some than for others, but all of them seemed to appreciate the chance to speak honestly with someone who was openly homosexual.

For myself, I learned a great deal about myself and about the Korean and Korean American community from this experience. It was a challenge for me to give up control of the group facilitation in this process. I typically facilitate such a class experience myself. In this instance I had to rely on my trust in the pastor, who was a heterosexual man, to convey my words to some of the group members. It was also clear that his co-facilitation would bridge the gender issues that were prevalent for some of the students. Like it or not, some of the students would be inclined to listen to me more with his presence as a male pastor authorizing my words. This was the right solution both educationally and culturally. Even though I was not in the dominant culture in that gathering, I belong to a racial group with privilege in this society and am a citizen of a country with a complicated history in Korea. Since I was invited as a guest into that context, there was a delicate balance to be achieved between the particular dominance of my social location in relation to them and the specific dominance of their social location as heterosexuals in relation to me as a lesbian.

The most important thing that happened in this multicultural teaching situation was that we each began to let go of our fear of the other as different; we began to understand those differences; and we sought ways to move toward a greater dialogue and understanding. We began a process of seeing the other more clearly, of being converted to perceiving the other as a complex human being and not a stereotype. Multicultural teaching, then, is often a process of the teacher facilitating a way for members of different social groups to turn toward one another in an open dialogue. But this facilitation was successful, in part, because we did not ignore the conflict that was inevitably a part of that teaching situation.

Seeing Clearly and Conflict

Seeing clearly is the discipline we need to develop for multicultural teaching that centers us squarely in our fear of someone who is extremely different from us. In theory we might have no issue with this statement. But in reality this discipline places us as teachers in the uncomfortable position of living through conflict and contention. Most of us do not relish the thought of being in such a position. In fact, we might have cause to wonder about persons who enjoy such conflict.

Attentiveness to the conflict that arises in diverse teaching settings most concretely reveals to us the discipline of seeing clearly. The fear of potential and actual conflict remains arguably the single most important obstacle to effective teaching in a multicultural context. This is not a phantom fear. Real conflicts erupt frequently in diverse educational settings. Many teachers feel fearful and powerless when tensions crack open during class. Such experiences, badly handled, can become an interfering obstacle to learning for both students and teachers, and in the most difficult cases can become a permanent barrier to any learning.

However, as teachers we must come to grips with the reality that *conflict, and its constructive management, is essential to a multicultural teaching context.* In fact, if we are teaching in a diverse setting and inter-group conflict is not being worked through on some level, then we can be certain that we are not engaging the diversity properly or teaching effectively. Multicultural teaching challenges us to handle the conflict so that it becomes a teachable moment for all the learners.

When members of different social groupings meet to engage in a learning process, authentic dialogue demands that the differences each group experiences become a part of the conversation. Without a clear discussion of the real distinctions of lived experience that affect each group in relation to the subject, no meaningful, in-depth dialogue can occur. The expression of those differences, along with the difficulty for some persons who do not experience those differences to understand what the other group lives, causes tensions that must be facilitated in the classroom.

Articulating the ways an obstacle affects us and our understanding of a subject matter can be a highly emotionally charged situation. The student is talking about more than an idea; she is talking about her life. Much more is at stake than making an intellectual point. If someone from another social location ignores her comment or treats it disrespectfully, a personalized conflict of genuine rage and intensity might occur. In many ways the student cannot be blamed completely for such a reaction, because in multicultural teaching, a person's sense of self is on the line, not just her opinion. Point of view and life experiences in these contexts overlap and blur any meaningful distinction between the two.[1]

I once had a college theology class on ecclesiology in which the professor, a Jesuit priest, spoke at great length about "those women" who wanted to be Catholic priests. He wondered why they did not understand that they could serve the church as lay women or women religious. This was in the late 1970s, when arguments for women priests in the Roman Catholic tradition were only just beginning to make inroads into the consciousness of the church. I remember the rage I felt at this priest, one whom I actually liked and respected as a thinker. I felt angry disagreement with his point of view as well as betrayal at his insensitivity. It was difficult to distinguish which was operating more—my intellectual disagreement or my emotional feeling of being oppressed and disempowered by his comments. When I challenged his point of view, pointing out that it was easy for him to take that position because he *was* a priest and it was not denied him, he responded in exactly the wrong way. He allowed that perhaps I had a point, but on his face he wore a bemused smile that revealed his true patronizing attitude and behavior. It was hard for me to separate my disagreement with his point of view and the real threat I felt as a woman from his belief. He was not just attacking my belief; he was attacking me.

A better way to handle my challenge would have been to try to be open to what I said by engaging it, challenging it, disagreeing with it, or even refuting it. Doing this in a respectful manner that takes seriously a student's point of view would be a key element to the encounter. Dismissing my point only intensified my feelings of being attacked. It was a teachable moment in which he could have facilitated a conversation in the class in which both sides of the issue could have been engaged openly.

When we see clearly, we do not run away from those conflictual moments when true dialogue and authentic learning become possible. But this demands ego strength and a centering of self that can be open to constructive conflict. It demands the ability to not personalize the challenge, that is, to see it in its broader social structural context. It also demands an ability to allow constructive anger to be a part of the conversation. Seeing clearly involves perceptive attentiveness to conflict as it emerges in group interaction and the anger that goes along with it.

Seeing Clearly and Anger

Anger need not be feared in a diverse teaching context. In fact, it is often a healthy sign that differences are being authentically raised between groups. Anger can also be a good sign that a marginalized group is pushing off victimization and openly resisting its disempowerment. Anger can be a sign of a passion for justice that is necessary in an inequitable society.[2] When we see clearly, we accept that honest engagement with others across boundaries of difference may at times include genuine anger.

However, anger that is not handled in a constructive manner can be destructive for all concerned. This is the anger that we should fear in a teaching setting—the uncontrolled rage that leads to no constructive solution. It descends into fighting and warring that has no discernible positive effect. Venting anger may relieve the feelings of rage, but it does nothing to address the underlying causes of the problem. Nor does it propose a strategy or solution. As teachers we should do whatever we can to prevent this type of brutalizing of one another.

It is important to understand, though, that expression of anger is culturally coded.[3] What is an acceptable mode of expression in one cultural group is a "mortal sin" in another. For example, an Italian American or Hispanic might have no problem with a loud, heated, emotional discussion, but a Chinese American might. This is part of the cultural conflict that a teacher must facilitate in a multicultural context. Seeing clearly means that we work hard to understand what the cultural expression of anger is in a group and how it is threatening to another group, perhaps even to ourselves. Part of constructive anger involves the teacher's ability to both honor it by giving it a fair hearing and use it strategically for learning.

I once negotiated an angry confrontation in class between a white woman and a black man. The subject of their conflict is less important for the point of this example than the actual process of the argument. The man was pressing the woman on the issue of white privilege in regards to discussing race and became very angry when she refused to respond to one of his questions. He saw that as the embodiment of white privilege, which in this context it seemed to be. She, on the other hand, shut down her communication because she felt that his approach was hostile to her. She clearly perceived it as hostile, and from the outside, his approach appeared aggressive.

When I intervened, I tried to get them to first understand the cultural coding of their communicative processes. He spoke about the ways in which raised voices, which sometimes were pointed and aggressive, were fairly common in his experience of black culture. She spoke about the ways in which that type of communication was perceived in her white, Anglo-Saxon

Protestant culture as not part of civil conversation and practically "immoral." I also tried to help them to bring to the surface the reality of the racist tensions that exist between black men and white women that make open communication problematic. She spoke of her previous history of sexual violence that caused her to be threatened around aggressive men. In the end, the best resolution we were able to arrive at was an uneasy cease-fire between the two of them. While their anger was never really resolved, it was at least able to stay controlled enough to be used more or less constructively in the educational process.

For my part, I struggled to find a balance between letting the anger be expressed and worked through toward an educational end, and not turning the class (and my subsequent individual interaction with them) into a therapy session. I tried to approach the conflict with several guidelines in mind. First, I did not avoid dealing with the conflict. In fact, I was actively involved in facilitating the conversation in class. The worst thing teachers can do in that situation is to pretend that nothing happened. It sends a message to our students, especially those from minority power groups, that their concerns are not important in the class dynamic. Second, I sought to help them see the larger issue of their cultural communication, rather than the specific issue over which they fought. Third, I sought to place squarely in the center of the discussion the social structural issues that were a significant part of the conflict and their anger. Fourth, I drew a very clear boundary on how long the fight could continue. Once we had made our way through aspects that were fundamentally about negotiating conflict in diversity, what remained were more individual issues that could have turned the discussion to group therapy. At that point I said that I was calling a halt to the discussion and that I would speak to the two students after class.

This example reveals the ways in which conflict is inherent to multicultural teaching settings and the anger that arises from these conflicts. What is important to remember is that the conflict and anger do not have to be problems in themselves. They are only problems when they are ignored or handled in a way that escalates them rather than resolves them.

Seeing Clearly and Conversion

Theologically speaking, the discipline of seeing clearly involves an attentiveness to conversion, that is, to turn away from fear of the other who is different and turn toward acceptance of differing worldviews and experiences. This conversion can be jarring, unsettling, and confusing; but it is the only way to begin to negotiate the tremendous diversity of a multicultural teaching context. It is a turning away from judgments about groups of people without understanding the complexities of their experiences of social structural and personal discrimination.

Conversion demands an unflinching look at ourselves as teachers. One critique of ourselves involves considering the conscious or unconscious stereotypes that are part of our teaching selves. What are the personal prejudices that we bring into our classrooms? Perhaps we believe we are beyond such biases. Looking at the assumptions we bring into the classroom can be quite revealing. For example, do we assume every Asian American or Hispanic student has trouble speaking English? Do we assume our students are heterosexual unless they self-declare their sexual orientation? Do we assume that Native American, African American, and Hispanic students come from situations of poverty? Do we assume that all men are insensitive to women and their needs? Assumptions are subtle and difficult to see without real effort. Yet they are inevitably part of the baggage we bring into any teaching situation.

Another critique we might subject ourselves to involves examining the ways in which, consciously or unconsciously, we universalize human experience and ignore the particularity of difference among and between groups. Do we assume our students see the world exactly as we do? Do we assume that they have the same values and the same perspectives as us? It takes conscious attentiveness and reflection to become more aware of these assumptions.

As difficult as it is to see personal prejudices, understanding social structural discrimination is even more complex. In this instance, if we are members of the privileged group, we may be blinded by our own experience of privilege. We can only begin to see the obstacles other groups face when we listen and understand their experiences from hearing their stories. The assumptions we bring to a teaching context about a social group are greatly influenced by what we do not know about their experience. Conversion in this instance means making a conscious effort to see the world beyond the narrowness of our own experience. At Union Seminary, where I teach, I frequently deal with the cognitive dissonance that occurs for many white, European American, Protestant, middle- or upper-class, heterosexual men who are overwhelmed in the environment of intense and challenging diversity. For these men, it is often the first time that they have experienced even realizing that different groups have different experiences, let alone been so overtly challenged about their social structural privilege. Many resist the realization that they experience privilege in this society.

My educational task involves helping these men lose some of their defensiveness so that they can listen and understand the varied experiences of privilege and marginalization they hear about in the readings and in class. A key factor for them is the degree of openness they have to the worldview of others who do not share their experiences of privilege. Seeing clearly—that is, turning away from fear and judgment of difference—allows a conversion to occur. This conversion entails realizing two aspects about themselves in an unjust social structure. The first involves understanding their own conscious or unconscious prejudices and assumptions about the lived experience of others and removing those prejudices and assumptions from their actions. The second aspect involves understanding that while they may not act with any overt prejudices, they benefit from the social privileges they have in a society of hegemonic power relations. This realization is important for all in a multicultural teaching context, but it is especially important for men from the dominant culture for whom unjust social relations can remain hidden, since they are, in large part, not the targets of them.

Seeing clearly, then, involves removing our fear of the other as different. This only happens when we engage the other authentically in honest dialogue. When the dialogue is an honest engagement, conflict inevitably develops in the teaching environment. It is the task of the teacher in this situation to facilitate the conflict toward a constructive learning between two groups who do not understand each other. The pedagogical task involves allowing the member of the minority group to be heard and helping the member of the dominant group to understand what he or she does not comprehend. Seeing clearly depends on a conversion to the other, to understanding and awareness of both personal prejudice and social structural difference that affects the other in different ways, depending on their social location to the dominant culture.

Learning to See Clearly

Seeing clearly is a function of how well we listen and understand the experiences of others. A conversion to another cannot be conjured. It is a grace from God. But we can seek to remain as open as we can to God's work in us that will make conversion possible.

One way that we can develop our ability to see clearly is to work very hard at the self-reflection and other-reflection that helps us to listen and understand others better. This means that we try to create a teaching practice that makes time for *reflection and evaluation.* The deeper we are able to engage our teaching practices, our inner selves, and our relationship to others, the more we will be able to see clearly in diverse teaching contexts. This is a major commitment to make in the overworked and overwhelmed lives of teachers. But without making time for reflection, we cannot make the space to be converted by the other.

A second way that we can develop our ability to see clearly builds directly upon the first suggestion. We need to provide *openness that allows God's Spirit to work in us,* so that we might experience a conversion to the other. Providing the openness to hear God's Spirit means not just creating the space and time for reflection on our teaching practice, but also allowing ourselves to be open to all that God is revealing to us about others and ourselves in that reflection process. Seeing clearly is the function of a personal and professional life that reflects deeply, discerns God's Word consistently, and remains open to the power of that Word to convert us fully. Forming a consistent openness helps us to develop the convictions that will guide us through multicultural teaching contexts.

Reflection on Teaching Practice

The complex nature of any teaching, but especially teaching in a pluralistic setting, demands a difficult balance. We need to rigorously critique our teaching competency and demand from ourselves our best performance. Yet we also need to forgive ourselves for those moments when we are not able to be as competent as we would like and for those moments when we are downright incompetent.

The ability to *forgive and be forgiven* is a fundamental skill, and theological theme, that we bring to multicultural teaching contexts. When we are part of the dominant cultural group in the setting, and we have spoken insensitively or unconsciously excluded someone from a marginalized group, we may feel the embarrassment of a job poorly done, but we might also feel the guilt of harming someone in their sense of self. We may feel paralyzed, seeking forgiveness from the injured person. This only exacerbates the tension. It is not up to the person/s from the marginalized group to absolve us from our guilt. Learning and forgiving in this context mean that we learn what the mistake was, resolve not to repeat it, and realize that we will only be trustworthy as teachers when we prove ourselves trustworthy. We forgive ourselves for our unconscious ignorance and let our changed actions rebuild our relationship with the injured group.

The dynamic of forgiveness is much more complicated when teachers are members of marginalized groups and experience hostility or insensitivity from our students. In those moments we are in the uncomfortable position of both having power as teacher and feeling disempowered as a member of a targeted group. It takes a remarkable amount of self-possession not to take personally a hostile or insensitive remark. It also takes wisdom to discern how to challenge the insensitivity or hostility and maintain an atmosphere of openness and learning. Such situations can easily degenerate into protracted power struggles between specific students and the teacher.

In these situations, forgiveness involves being clear about the issues at hand. Without doubt, hostility toward teachers cannot be tolerated, both on the level of a teacher's personhood and on the level of the teacher's authority in the classroom. In those instances, a firm boundary must be set indicating that the hostile behavior will not be tolerated. Only when the offending behavior is stopped can the teacher begin to forgive the learner and try to understand the reason for the hostility. Forgiveness in this circumstance seeks ways to both protect self and understand the motivation of the other.

With the issue of insensitivity due to lack of knowledge, it is easier to let our "teacher-self" be in control. Although the insensitive remark is painful or makes us angry, we can challenge it openly and make it a learning moment for the student and the class as a whole. It is not that we feel any less hurt, angry, irritated, or "sick and tired" of the inability of members of the dominant culture to understand and act in more sensitive ways. The difference between hostility and unintentional insensitivity speaks to motivation, and deliberate motivation to hurt is a much more problematic dynamic. Forgiveness in this instance means having the patience to endure while protecting self, and helping learners see the contradictions, insensitivities, and inaccuracies of their statements or actions.

Ultimately, I believe that forgiveness is both an act of will and a grace from God. There are many times as teachers when we would like to lash out at a student, especially if we are members of a minority grouping of any kind. Keeping in mind that learners are in our class precisely because they need to learn helps to deflect the pain and insult that we may feel.

1. Have you ever been "caught" in incorrect assumptions about a student or a group of students in a teaching context? How did you handle it? Are you satisfied with your response? What would you do differently if you had to do it again?

2. Consider a teaching experience where you had to forgive yourself for not handling a conflict over diversity well. What do you regret most about your performance? What have you learned from this event? How can you do it differently next time?

3. Consider a teaching experience in which you, as the teacher, experienced conflict as a member of a social structural minority group. In what way was your authority either consciously or unconsciously undermined? How did you handle the situation? What would you do differently if it were to happen again? Were you able to forgive the offending party? What did that forgiveness look like?

4

Acting Differently

During graduate school I taught two summer courses at a Jesuit liberal arts university. One course was an overview of feminist theology for an undergraduate audience. When I entered the room on the first night, I was surprised and pleased at the number of students in the course, especially the number of men. I had correctly assumed that most of the students were there because it fit their schedule and satisfied one course of their theology requirement. While this was true for both the men and the women in this course, it was especially true for the men. We would be meeting for five weeks, in two three-hour sessions per week. We would be spending intense time together, and I wondered how it would all turn out. How would I work with them on the contentious issues of feminist theology when, for most of them, their main motivation for the course was convenience?

The group was primarily white ethnic Roman Catholics from working-class and middle-class backgrounds, with one exception. One student was an African male who said he was interested in the topic because it was so utterly foreign to him. The gender composition was roughly half men and half women.

71

Some students had done previous coursework in theology, but for many it was their first exposure.

I decided that it would be educationally imperative to spend the early sessions helping the students understand what was at issue in feminist theology. I wanted to pose the problem so that they could see the contradictions present in texts and interpretations. I wanted them to begin the course by seeing the ways in which the experiences of many different women were left out of many types of social discourse. I decided, then, to begin the first class with a fishbowl experience. In this instructional strategy volunteers enter a small group in the front of the class and begin to have a discussion among themselves. The remainder of the group is invited to listen in on the conversation that is occurring in the front. In this instance I first asked for five male volunteers and put forward this question for them to discuss among themselves: "What was your experience of high school?"

Some of the males in the fishbowl looked at me as if I was crazy to ask such a question, while others looked pleadingly at me with eyes that said, "Can't you just lecture at us?" Eventually there were a few halting responses, mainly positive, about times of less responsibility, lots of sports, and helpful mentors. The group was clearly being self-protective and chose not to discuss any difficult or problematic experiences. After several painstaking minutes, which I am sure felt like an eternity to them, one member of the group looked at me and said, "Are we through yet?" On that note I thanked them for braving the experience and asked for female participants for the second fishbowl.

As you might expect, this next fishbowl was an entirely different experience than the first. The female participants were eager to talk about their experiences of high school. They spoke about the ways in which high school was very difficult for them. They spoke of the lack of mentors, feeling discriminated against and unheard in the classroom, hating the pressure they felt from boys to look a certain way and to "dumb down" or be rejected. This conversation set off a huge conflict among the men in the class. For many of them, including the African man, it was the first time it had occurred to them that women and men have different experiences of privilege and marginalization, and they did not want to believe it. It was, of course, still necessary to help them to see the variables of race, class, and sexuality in their understanding of difference, but it was important that they see the differences that existed in this ostensibly monocultural group.

The cognitive dissonance[1] was educationally important because it helped these men begin to understand that experience is not universal. But the process of resolving this cognitive dissonance was painstaking for them as students and for me as a female teacher. Many of the white male students were aggressive toward me for the first four sessions (twelve hours of class time). In each session I found ways pedagogically to pose the problem of gender (inclusive of race, class, sexual orientation) and the exclusion of women's experiences, letting the material speak for itself. The contradictions were difficult to deny, but many of the male students did. The African male student saw the contradictions, but he understood the controversy as an issue involving the difference between American and African worldviews about gender. He seemed to dismiss the issue as an American concern and seemed unable to see any problematic issues of gender in his own context, even though I sought to explain it in more global ways.

Honestly, it was difficult as a woman to do battle with these men for three hours twice a week. It seemed that we would be stuck at an impasse for the entire five weeks of the course. I struggled to keep my teacher-self in the forefront of my action. I kept searching for ways to help them understand better without turning the class over to them. I did not want to ignore the women in the class in order to resolve this conflict. I constantly stated to the men, "I am not saying that you have to agree with this theological point of view, but I am saying that you have to at least know that it exists and understand its main points."

I often wonder what helped me keep my composure during those difficult early days of that course. Besides grace, I think that a significant motivation for me was solidarity with the other women in the room and a desire to advocate on their behalf. As the instructor, I had a measure of power in that context that no other woman had. I knew how I felt about the issues, having had lots of time to read and think about them. The women students in the class were only beginning to find their voices on this issue. Many felt too threatened to speak too forcefully. There was a significant difference between what they wrote in their papers and what they felt able to contribute in class discussion. I made the decision to be in the forefront, so that the men could publicly fight with me on the issues of God-language and patriarchal bias in text and tradition, and not necessarily fight with the other women in the class. Clearly, the students had conversations with one another during the break and outside of class where the issues continued to be discussed. But at least in that public arena of the classroom, I was able to advocate for them by taking the brunt of the hostility.

What I found was that gradually the women became more empowered and spoke up for themselves, allowing me to recede into the background of the discussion. Also, many of the men were becoming more comfortable with the material and less threatened. As a strategy with the male students, I listened carefully to their protests, then consistently pointed out the contradiction between what they wanted to believe was true with the facts that they were seeing in the experience of women (both in the class discussion and in the readings). In the end those facts, combined with my insistence that they did not have to agree with a feminist point of view but that they had to know about it accurately, seemed to change the intense hostility from many of the men.

Patience with the educational process, creating safe space for the women in the room, and giving the men space to process their cognitive dissonance all came together to create a marvelous pedagogical experience. What began with hostility and contention ended in genuine dialogue. It is not that everyone agreed, or that all were converted to a feminist consciousness. Rather, we were able to discuss the readings with a real attempt to understand the different experiences that men and women of diverse cultural contexts have in relation to religion. Emotional patience as well as pedagogical design allowed me, through the readings and discussions, to open up issues of race, class, and sexuality, as well as gender. As a teacher, it helped me to open up a world for the students that they had not been exposed to before. In the end it was an immensely satisfying, although exhausting, experience.

I believe that what helped me to manage that pedagogical context was a strong conviction about the need to align myself with the targeted group, of which I was also a member, as we struggled to find our empowerment on the issue. The conviction involved attentiveness to my personal discomfort and the way it affected my teaching. The conviction also involved incorporating the spirituality of a critical mind and a discerning heart into my life as a teacher so that it affected my pedagogical practice. I was able in that instance to incorporate a way of seeing the world that understood my own marginalization, the marginalization of others, and a social analysis into my teaching so that I could act in a way that embodied my convictions.

My presence in that teaching context was complex. On the one hand, I was the teacher with all of the power that the role gives. I could have deflected the conflict in any number of ways. I could have absented myself from the fray and let the men and women of the class fight it out alone. Or I could have just lectured in a manner that entertained no discussion. None of these would have been pedagogically effective, but they were options for action. As the teacher I had the power to control the class dynamics in any way that I chose. On the other hand, I was a woman having to hear the same insults and insensitivities that the other women in the room had to hear. I was not personally immune from the feelings of anger and hurt that were generated from insensitive or outright sexist statements. I was challenged in that setting to act in a way that was pedagogically effective, personally protective, and morally grounded in my value system.

The complexity of my teaching presence might be reduced to a paradoxical situation. On the one hand, in the context of the class and the university structure, I had the majority of the power, but within the larger context of the social groups that were represented in that room, I was a member of a targeted, disempowered group. I both had power and had my power undermined. I both had authority and had my authority challenged. Also, I personally brought a set of values about just relationships between groups of people that influenced my actions. All in all, I was in a complicated set of power relations for which there is no easy recipe for appropriate action.

And yet part of the anxiety of teaching involves the reality that, in spite of all the complexity of the context—that, frankly, we would rather study for a period of time—we have to "show up" and act. That is, teachers do not have the luxury of waiting to act when things are clearer. We have a responsibility to come to class, do our jobs, and work through the complexity in the action-reflection of our teaching practice. Being clear about the convictions we bring to our teaching can help us navigate through this sort of complicated set of power relations.

Acting differently involves incorporating the disciplines of listening and understanding and seeing clearly, so that our teaching praxis demonstrably changes. Acting differently forms convictions in teachers that ground us morally and pedagogically. Convictions embody the worldview and value orientation we bring to any teaching context. They are the conscious and unconscious assumptions that we live with and act from in our teaching practice. They are both ubiquitous and unseen. They are the way our teaching selves become embodied in our teaching practice. The convictions we bring into a multicultural teaching context will affect our pedagogical actions.

Convictions and Syllabi

Convictions are revealed as the ways in which we can act differently because we have listened and understood diverse groups and have seen clearly what their life experience is in a society of unjust power relations. The incorporation of this "conversion to the other" forms the convictions that guide our approach to teaching in a multicultural context. A teacher who possesses a critical mind and a discerning heart lives out these convictions in an embodied way.

One of the most concrete expressions of our convictions is in the syllabus for a course.[2] In that document we articulate for our students all that we are convicted about in regards to the subject content, the evaluative process, and the instructional strategy. The syllabus is never a neutral document because it represents our personal take on the subject matter and the way we believe it should be communicated.

Issues of inclusion and exclusion in a syllabus' content are significant for teachers in multicultural contexts. Whose voice we hear and whose voice is left out speaks volumes about our convictions. If we have cultivated a teaching character that has sought to change our understanding so that we comprehend more fully the experiences of those who are different from us, then we must concretize that understanding in the way that we present material.

The discipline of acting differently forces us to ensure that our beliefs and actions cohere in our syllabus construction. A familiar difficulty in the process of becoming more multiculturally sensitive as teachers involves a disconnection between what we know in theory and what we do in practice. For example, a common problem for teachers from the dominant culture is having a conviction about the need to be more inclusive of the voices of people of color, yet seeing them as an addition to the "real" subject matter of the discipline, which, of course, is all white and Western European. Consciously or unconsciously, the knowledge base of the academic discipline becomes understood as fixed in its canon. That canon almost always contains voices that are predominantly white male, with perhaps a smattering of white women, and decidedly Western European in flavor. The addition of excluded voices in the syllabus is viewed as a major liberalizing of the content structure of the course. Yet the point of view of the course remains white and Western European.

Acting differently in regards to syllabus construction means that we ensure that the diversity of voices we include changes the way we construct the knowledge base that we teach. It is not enough, for example, to talk about the contributions of women of color in one class session. Rather, taking our convictions seriously means that we allow those voices to *change the way we understand the subject matter* and then incorporate that understanding into our primary communication to students.

I once had a discussion with a white feminist colleague whose academic specialty was biblical studies about womanist approaches to the Bible, such as the methods developed by several African American women biblical scholars. I asked her how she used those approaches in her courses. She told me that "she did not do that method" and, therefore, did not use it in class. I was stunned. This colleague was an ardent feminist, generally quite knowledgeable about race issues, yet she could not see the ways in which womanist approaches to the Bible would be important for an introductory-level Bible course. We had a long talk about this contradiction, and it became clear that she was unconsciously trapped between her own convictions and the dominant understanding of "real" content in the Bible. Challenging this notion of what is "real" content would have likely put her at odds with the power structure of her field. But it is a risk that would be necessary to take in order for her convictions and her teaching practice to integrate. In the end she was able to see the problems with her understanding and create a more inclusive syllabus.

Convictions and Instructional Strategies

Specific instructional strategies comprise another concrete expression of our convictions as teachers. In a diverse teaching context, the instructional strategies we use can aid or impede learning, often in quite specific ways. A discussion that genuinely dialogues across boundaries of difference can foster an open environment where students learn about one another and diverse points of view. A discussion that discourages diverse points of view can create tremendous conflict in a multicultural teaching context.

Instructional strategies are the specific teaching techniques that we use to implement a lesson.[3] If we have a conviction about the importance of educational equity for all in a learning environment, then in a diverse teaching setting we need to pay serious attention to the ways in which the instructional strategies aid or impede learning for various social groups of students. Our own attentive observations can be a guide for action. In a lecture, what questions are being asked and by which students? Who seems disconnected from the logical flow of the lecture? In a discussion, who is speaking and who is not speaking? Are women hesitant to speak? Are the male students dominating the conversation? Are students from one racial or ethnic group silent or dominating the conversation?

Teaching contexts that include students for whom English is not their first language present an important consideration in pedagogy for multicultural education. Several years ago a colleague and I had a helpful challenge from a group of Korean students in a class on pedagogical practices. We were teaching the students how to use the case study instructional strategy. In this technique, groups in the class debate an issue in order to clarify specific aspects that are under discussion. While implementing this technique, we were aware of some tension and discomfort among the Korean students. When we evaluated the process at the end of the session with the class, the Korean students challenged us about this instructional strategy from the perspective of their cultural context. They told us that the debate format was disempowering to them in several ways. First, as non-native English speakers they found the spontaneous dialogue necessary for case study work difficult to manage. They could not easily keep up with the pace of the conversation. Second, direct, face-to-face debate was extremely uncomfortable for them, because they were used to less direct interactions. Finally, they reminded us that for many years during the military dictatorship in Korea (when many of them were college students), it was literally life-threatening to debate issues openly. This important discussion helped us see the ways our instructional strategy impeded the learning for this group of international students, and it helped us to design a more useful one.

Learning to Act Differently

Forming convictions and living out of them in integrated ways helps us to incorporate new ways of understanding our students in all of their diversity. Convictions result from both analytic rigor and spiritual reflection on our lives and teaching practices. Who we are and the deep-seated beliefs that we bring to the classroom must be one. This is essential for any teaching context. Diversity, with its complicated set of multiple relationships, makes that identity formation that much more complex.

There are several ways we can learn to solidify our convictions as teachers in multicultural contexts. These suggestions are largely dependent on spiritually entering into a stance of a critical mind and a discerning heart, which helps us learn, understand, and see more clearly.

One way to learn to act differently is to understand our *motivation*. Examining our motivation can help us to uncover our beliefs and to see how they are operating in our teaching. When we discover what moves us, we get a clearer glimpse of what values undergird our action.

For example, are we motivated to display our knowledge, or are we motivated to help students learn? When teaching is about displaying our knowledge, we are teaching only out of our own needs. Insecurity is our motivation. This can cause a serious contradiction between our convictions and our teaching praxis. Convictions that live openly in our lives, rather than in our statements alone, are formed from a secure self. When we are emotionally secure as people and as teachers, the needs of the learners can be our more likely motivation.

Another way to learn to act differently is to examine rigorously *whether or not we believe in what we are doing.* We can only teach well if we believe in what we are teaching. If the subject matter is meaningless or irrelevant, or if the point of view of the content is problematic or offensive without critical examination, then our teaching competency will be affected. More to the point, if we do not believe in what we are teaching, then we must ask ourselves what we *do* believe. This process can help us form our convictions in more genuinely honest and meaningful ways. We can grow from the convictions we think we have to the convictions we authentically have, thereby discovering our beliefs more clearly. Perhaps our convictions were never really formed, or perhaps we are entering an intellectual and emotional transition in which our convictions are being uprooted and new ones are taking their place. Genuinely believing in what we are teaching can help to ensure that our convictions ground our teaching practice.

Reflection on Teaching Practice

Pedagogical practice includes the presentation of the self to the learner. Through the self, we communicate the material to be learned and the process of learning it. No authentic teaching can exist without the ability to relate to learners as people. Teaching without the ability to be in relationship is like operating a machine without lubrication—movement is next to impossible.

In multicultural teaching contexts the ability to relate across boundaries of difference is a fundamental skill. We learn to cross boundaries of difference in part through reading and education, but also from our ability to relate to those who are different from us. Some teachers get paralyzed in multicultural contexts because we find it difficult to relate to our students who have different experiences. Sometimes teachers cannot relate due to a lack of knowledge or to misunderstanding, but more often the inability to relate is rooted in *fear*. In many ways, then, the spirituality of multicultural teaching is dependent on our ability to work through our prejudices and fears of those who are different from us.

This is a very difficult task in many ways. There are often genuine reasons why we are afraid of other groups. Perhaps I am a woman who has been a victim of sexual violence, and I am therefore uncomfortable around men. Perhaps I am a Puerto Rican man who has been verbally abused or been the victim of white violence, and I am therefore defensive and fearful. Perhaps I am a white, heterosexual, upper-class man who has been confronted many times by members of minority groups. In short, the conflicted nature of our social interactions creates real reasons for fear and defensiveness.

But teachers do not have the luxury of staying in these fears. We have a responsibility as people in society but also as members of the teaching profession to deal with our fears, prejudices, anger, and insecurities, so that they do not interfere with our interaction with learners. We must work through those issues that are obstacles to our ability to communicate with learners and form relationships with them.

As in every multicultural teaching context, our social location plays a significant role in the ways we experience fear, prejudice, or even threat. If we are part of a minority power group, the abuses and insensitivities we experience in society, let alone in the classroom, can make us defensive or aggressive. We must find ways to resist the prejudices hurled at us, challenge unconscious insensitivities, and overcome our fears, or we will not be able to teach effectively. The more secure we can be in our identity, our worth, and our ability to protect ourselves, the better able we will be to deal with hostile undermining.

If we are part of the dominant power group, the angry challenges directed at us and the realization of our privilege at the expense of others can make us defensive, threatened, and paralyzed with guilt. We must find ways to not personalize the justified rage of marginalized persons. We must take the guilt that belongs to our behavior and the privileges we receive and allow expression of anger. We must learn to accept challenge and change our point of view and our action. We must learn to deal with our conscious and unconscious issues of supremacy over minority groups. The more secure we are in ourselves, and the more we have dealt with our issues of supremacy, fear, and prejudice, the more effectively we will be able to teach in a multicultural context.

Fear challenges our convictions deep in our being. When we confront our fears and work through them, we help to strengthen our convictions. Our convictions ground us in a diverse teaching context, and with that grounding we can better relate to all of the students before us.

1. When you face yourself honestly, what group of persons do you feel most uncomfortable with in the classroom? What is the reason for your discomfort? How can you begin to work through your discomfort?

2. How do you tend to handle conflict in a teaching setting? Is it different from the ways you handle it in other settings? What would you like to do differently in the way you handle conflict? How can you learn to do it?

3. Think of a time in your teaching experience when your convictions carried you through a difficult class experience. How were those convictions formed in you? Were your convictions affirmed, challenged, or changed from the experience?

4. Who or what supports you in contentious teaching situations? What resources do you draw from to carry you through?

5. What motivates you to teach? What do you feel most urgent about in your teaching? How is this expressed in your culture? How do you think persons from a different culture experience this?

5

Staying Faithful

Like so many in the week following the catastrophic attack on the World Trade Center, I felt the need to go downtown, to get as close as I could get to lower Manhattan and "Ground Zero." I sought to go not as a voyeur in a crisis, but rather as a silent witness to the enormity of what happened there the week before.

I was one of the many pilgrims on Sunday morning, September 16, 2001, walking along Canal Street—that was as close as we could get to "Ground Zero" at that time. Some were praying in groups. Some were walking with flowers. Some were milling around, seemingly trying to blend into the atmosphere of grief. Others were just going about their business —knowing it was anything but business as usual.

At the corner of Canal and West Broadway I paused for a long while—seeing smoke and heavy vehicles—mostly trying to comprehend as fully as I was able what was *not* there. At the corner of Canal and Sixth Avenue I stopped and looked up again. In the past those two towers loomed over the landscape for me, especially from that vantage point. A stranger passed me and said, "They're not there, are they?" "No," I said. "It's shocking." We nodded in sad, silent agreement. As I made my way up Sixth Avenue, I was overwhelmed at all of the signs of collective grieving that I saw: posters of loved ones missing, a fire station that lost eleven firefighters, candles and flowers at every corner—shrines of heartache and an urgent, pleading hope.

A particular sign caught my attention at Bleecker Street. It quoted a version of Romans 8:31: "If God is for us, who can be against us?" Someone had written on the sign a commentary to that biblical verse: "They acted in the name of God as well. Will you do as they do?" To which someone else responded in large, black letters: "Yes!" Finally, another responded to that emphatic statement: "Then you are as they are. You will kill innocents."

This debating street graffiti stayed with me all day on that Sunday and rolled around in my heart as I prepared a sermon for later that week at Union's weekday chapel service. It seemed to me that the debate that I saw on the poster represented a deeper conversation: a conversation about who we are as a diverse people, how we are to act in a multicultural society, and what kind of education can lead us on this path.

These are the types of questions we must ask ourselves. A spirituality of multicultural teaching seeks to form teachers who possess a conviction and a commitment to train students to be responsible participants in a multicultural world. As teachers in multicultural contexts, we create learning environments that are in many ways a microcosm of our larger society. The way in which we operate in our classrooms models for students ways to behave and ways to deal with conflicts in the larger diverse society. By our actions we are teaching our students either functional or dysfunctional ways of living in the inevitable conflicts of a multicultural world.

During a time in human history when the tensions of living in a diverse world pose both challenge and possibility, effective multicultural teaching becomes not only an important commitment but also an urgent necessity.

In this final chapter I want to talk about the endurance necessary for a spirituality of multicultural teaching. The change of heart and mind I am advocating is the task of a lifetime. It requires staying faithful to the spiritual disciplines of listening and understanding, seeing clearly, and acting differently. It requires a *commitment* to the necessity of relating to and understanding those who are "other" to us, the *courage* to face our limitations of knowledge and experience of groups different from us, and the *patience* to engage in the ongoing process of intercultural understanding and communication. These are the elements that ground a critical mind and a discerning heart for the long haul.

Commitment

Knowing, relating to, and understanding those who have different experiences from us constitutes a fundamental necessity in the diverse, global world in which we live. We cannot claim to be properly educated ourselves, or to be effective teachers, if we do not seek to understand the plurality of peoples and experiences that make up the human community. By effective teaching, I mean the ability to communicate knowledge to students in ways that are culturally appropriate and in which various learning styles are honored.

As such, this commitment to engage and open ourselves to be changed through encounters with others involves a desire to become a complete human being. Knowing about other cultures is not merely adding exotic experiences to our worldview; rather, we cannot know reality fully without knowing the plurality of groups in our world. An important caveat must be stated clearly here. While it is essential to know other cultures, it is just as essential to ask ourselves *why* we want to know about other cultures. Are we learning about other cultures in order to exploit, control, and commodify them? In many ways empires sought to understand the cultures they colonized for just such reasons. This awareness cautions us against uncritical appropriation of other cultural norms and histories without a corresponding commitment to social justice and political empowerment.

We live in an age with sophisticated technology that allows us a global reach to other cultures in terms of travel and communication at breakneck speed. Although we can reach across the globe, this has not necessarily come with increased understanding of other cultures. For example, in the wake of the terrorist attacks of 9/11, there were a frightening number of attacks not only against Muslims but also against those of Middle Eastern heritage and anyone who resembled them, including African Americans. The existential crisis that the terrorist attacks brought about in the United States reveals the ignorance and misunderstanding about Islam and the role of the United States in the Islamic world. Of course, this is not the first time for such reactions in American history. Our history records similar treatment of Japanese Americans and other Asian Americans during World War II. Our global interactiveness will only increase our exposure to other cultures. Multiculturalism will become more and more the reality of our country, not just in our big cities. Educators must respond to this reality and reaffirm our commitments to learn about other cultures and to teach in ways that are culturally sensitive.

Courage

Most teachers understand that learning constitutes a process and that all processes take their own time. But often a curious paradox exists. While we accept that learning is a process for our students, we might have trouble accepting that learning to teach more successfully is a process for ourselves. We learn through critical reflection on our teaching practices ways to be more effective in the classroom, but for many of us there are clear limitations regarding what we are willing to attempt and what we assiduously avoid pedagogically.

On one level, all of us can be excused from culpability for protecting ourselves from being overly exposed in our limitations. Truly, the act of teaching demands an exposure of self that can be unnerving. But the fact remains that learning to teach effectively in any context, especially in a multicultural context, demands a developmental learning process that we might not be able to accept in ourselves.

Perhaps we can better accept the developing nature of our teaching skills in multicultural contexts when, to begin with, we feel comfortably competent as teachers. It is difficult to tolerate our limitations as teachers when those limitations make us feel vulnerable. Feeling inept or as if we are unable to perform at a basic level of competence makes it literally impossible to enter the classroom in a way that engages the students or interacts with them.

Perhaps we shy away from the challenges of teaching in a more multiculturally responsive way because on some level we feel incompetent doing it. It seems easier in those moments to teach from what we know, even if it might not be helpful for a significant portion of the class. The potential conflicts of teaching in a way that acknowledges diversity in the classroom can seem overwhelming and, therefore, difficult to face. As teachers we know how difficult it can be at times to try to communicate with students who come from the same world and set of experiences as us. Attempting to communicate across the boundaries of different experiences can seem overwhelming and threatening.

This is one of the reasons why multicultural teaching involves more than just teaching technique. Because it deals so relentlessly with feelings of vulnerability and limitations in us as human beings and as teachers, it demands a spiritual grounding, a habit of mind and heart, that helps us to move the act of teaching away from our own ego needs and toward the learning we hope to effect. Multicultural teaching demands the courage to face the limitations of what we know and understand about those who are other to us, and to learn to teach in a different way. Multicultural teaching demands the courage to engage in a developmental learning process of our own pedagogical proficiency.

In many ways, multicultural teaching involves the risk of learning new ways of operating in the classroom with diverse groups of students. What are some ways to help us find the courage to face any limitations we might bring as teachers to the task of multicultural teaching? First of all, it is essential that we develop our communication skills. Confidence in our ability to communicate with our students, and to sort out issues and conflicts, builds courage. In a multicultural teaching context we must be willing to wade into a constructive conflict and help resolve it so that learning occurs.

Second, we need to develop an analytic ability to examine the dynamics of a class, rather than personalizing what students say or do. Seeking to comprehend what students are trying to communicate through their comments or actions can give us the courage to find ways to negotiate a conflict that needs to happen.

Third, we can inform ourselves about diverse cultures—our own and those that have different experiences from us. There is no substitute for knowing the history of a group, learning about their lived reality in society, and understanding their cultural norms, communication style, and learning styles.

Fourth, we need to have a clear sense of our authority as teacher in the classroom and our responsibility to take leadership to help focus the group learning in a constructive direction. We gain courage from awareness of our professional responsibility to ensure that class dynamics function so all can feel safe and empowered.

Finally, courage comes from faith in the God who leads us into the ministry of teaching. This vocational clarity about the importance of teaching as a ministry of service keeps us able to faithfully stay in the act of teaching, even when feeling overwhelmed.

Patience

In the futuristic science fiction movie *The Matrix,* two of the main characters, Trinity and Neo, find themselves needing to escape a dangerous situation. Their only means of transportation out of their circumstances is a helicopter, which neither knows how to operate. With a phone call, Trinity is able to get the pilot program for the helicopter wired into her head. Within seconds, she becomes an expert pilot. As much as we might like it to be so, learning how to teach in multicultural classrooms is not as instantaneous as this!

Effective teaching in a multicultural context demands patience as we engage in the ongoing process of intercultural learning. We learn about other cultures through reading, dialogue, and the lived experience of interacting with others. Patience emerges from our ability to accept that we cannot know everything right away. At the same time, we do know something about teaching inclusively. We know how to structure a learning task so that the needs of all the members can be addressed. And if we don't structure it appropriately, we know that we can make adjustments so that we can teach inclusively. There are certain fundamental questions we as teachers ask ourselves in teaching contexts:

• Who are the students?
• Who is participating or not participating and why?
• How can we focus the discussion or provide examples that relate better to their experiences?
• What are the students' barriers to learning?

The goal of these questions is to understand better who they are and how they learn. Teachers also need to ask ourselves what we need to learn in order to teach a particular group better next time.

• What don't I know about this group?
• How can I find it out?
• What do I observe about them and about me as I teach this group?

Time, reflection, and experience build patience. If we can trust the process and stay faithful to its discipline, we can learn to be patient with it and ourselves.

Conclusion

Critical Minds, Discerning Hearts, and the Hospitable Classroom

In this work, I have sought to articulate a spiritual attentiveness that forms both a critical mind and a discerning heart. A critical mind has the capacity to see social structural realities, and a discerning heart has the capacity to see individuals with empathy and compassion. A critical mind and a discerning heart are formed through three movements: listening and understanding, seeing clearly, and acting differently. These movements ground a critical mind and a discerning heart in comprehension, conversion, and conviction.

Spiritual attentiveness that forms a critical mind and a discerning heart exists most fruitfully in a hospitable environment. Therefore, hospitality is an important contextual component in the spirituality of multicultural teaching. Ana María Pineda defines the Christian practice of hospitality as "the practice of providing a space where the stranger is taken in and known as the one who bears gifts."[1] This way of thinking shows two very important truths of a diverse world of interdependent peoples: We need to engage those who are "strangers" to us, and we must do so from an understanding that they bring resources, skills, and knowledge valuable for all. From this perspective of engagement of others and respect for the gifts they bring, we can consider ways to develop a hospitable classroom. As teachers, grounding ourselves in these truths can be an appropriate starting point.

Creating a sense of *welcome inclusion* is one component of a hospitable classroom. When we welcome someone into a space, we do it cordially and respectfully, with an openness that makes that person feel that he or she is wanted. We indicate that we wish to share our resources as well as ourselves. Hospitality is the positive disposition we have to invite others into the environment we create. As Lynne Westfield reminds us, "Hospitality is an attitude."[2]

But welcome alone is not enough in a teaching context. Welcome must be paired with inclusion, that is, making that person and her concerns a part of the class experience. For example, inviting gay, lesbian, bisexual, and transgendered persons to be open in a learning setting means not only creating space for their physical presence but also incorporating their experiences into the content and discussion.

Welcome inclusion that develops hospitable classrooms goes beyond including specific persons that happen to be present. Rather, it seeks to create an intellectual openness to knowledge that is inclusive of many perspectives. If we create a history course in which every reading and point of view culturally reflects white European or European American men, then we are not creating a spirit of welcome inclusion. In a diverse classroom we create hospitality, in part through our openness to integrate a diversity of perspectives into the ways we construct a course.

It is important to keep in mind the culturally coded nature of what constitutes welcome inclusion. Different cultures understand hospitality in different ways. In the classroom, this reality must be negotiated. Teachers who seek to create hospitable classrooms must engage the variety of cultural expectations around hospitality that are present in the group. What is hospitable to some cultures may seem inhospitable to others. The realities of power differences in a society of inequities make awareness of the cultural coding of welcome inclusion especially imperative. If a teacher from the dominant culture uncritically imposes his or her own cultural notions of hospitality on the group, then only some students will benefit from the hospitality offered. For others it might, in fact, prove to be alienating.

Understanding the variety of culturally defined notions of hospitality thus becomes part of creating a sense of welcome inclusion. For example, Westfield notes that constitutive elements of a womanist practice of hospitality are intimacy, reciprocity, and safety.[3] For some cultures the intimacy of this type of hospitality might be overwhelming, while for others it might be empowering. As another example, in the Korean American community monthly gatherings consisting of Bible study, worship, and prayer form an educational community of outreach and incorporation. The "ricing community"[4] (the metaphor they use to denote hospitality as a fundamental component of their community) creates hospitality, mutual nurture, and inclusion in the Korean American community that attends to the constant influx of immigrants. Understanding the convergence of educational, social, historical, and religious aspects of hospitality would be important in creating a sense of welcome inclusion for students from this community.

Another aspect of a hospitable classroom involves establishing a sense of *safety* for all participants. We begin by acknowledging the limits of safety in a classroom context. Students bring into class the social relationships that they experience in the world outside of the class. We must remember, therefore, that safety can be a relative term. A Latina colleague once told me that classroom safety was a relative term for her because she could never completely remove from a group setting the social reality of discrimination that exists outside of that teaching context.

Understanding the limits allows for considering ways to create a sense of safety in a hospitable classroom. We can attempt to develop learning environments that are welcoming, inclusive, and honoring of each person's needs. This occurs when we ensure that each person feels free to engage fully and raise his or her concerns openly. Learners need to feel that the context affirms the reality of difference and, therefore, it is possible to challenge behaviors and comments that are offensive or threatening. Learners must have the safety to feel that they can challenge another without losing a sense of their own self–identity. A sense of safety is built, in part, by creating an environment in which it is possible to challenge threats to one's sense of personhood. Teachers create a sense of safety from their capacity to facilitate the group interaction in a way that respects a student's need to feel secure in an educational setting.

Honoring the needs and concerns of the class often involves creating the space for *honest dialogue* and is another aspect of a hospitable classroom. When we create the possibility for honest dialogue, we create the space for both challenge and affirmation. Students need to feel free to contend with one another over the inevitable conflicts that are part of an inequitable social structure. At the same time there needs to be space for affirmation of the ways in which we have learned to understand one another better and have engaged one another more authentically.

The creation of a hospitable classroom is a mutual accountability of all the group members. However, as the ones who are authorized to be responsible for the learning experience, teachers bear an important role in the creation of a hospitable classroom. *Teachers use the power that they have to host the learners present.* When we welcome someone into our home, hospitality happens because the host is responsible for attending to the details of space, food, environment, and social interactions for the specific people who will be present that make for ease and openness together. The same is true in the classroom. Teachers attend to the details of group dynamics and pedagogical design that make the learning experience one in which students feel at ease and open to engagement.

An important caveat involves understanding that hospitality freely offered cannot be imposed on students. For many students who come from communities or groups that experience social discrimination, receiving hospitality from any authority figure, especially if he or she is from the dominant culture, can expose them to interactions that might feel threatening. We must understand the ways in which engaging in the hospitable classroom that we seek to create can involve risk for students from marginalized groups. In some instances the risk might be the fear of invisibility or isolation, either from being ignored outright or from being tokenized—each of which are hurtful and humiliating. The teacher who acts as host in the multicultural classroom must allow space for trust to be developed over time, so that engagement of the hospitality is freely chosen.

The hospitality that we create must also be extended to ourselves as teachers. We must be able to receive hospitality from ourselves and others, or we will never be able to give it. We need to create an inner experience of welcome, inclusion, safety, challenge, and affirmation. We do this through developing a centered teaching-self that reflects deeply on our teaching practices and connects fully with colleagues and mentors who support and affirm us.

The capacity to give and receive hospitality is, in many ways, the wellspring of our engagement in a multicultural world as teachers. We learn about others who are different from us when they agree to let us into their world and experience. It is their willingness to risk hospitality with us that allows us to learn about who they are, what their history has been, and what their experiences of life have taught them. At the same time, it is our capacity to offer hospitality that creates an openness to risk the engagement at all. Hospitality is a deeply mutual spiritual practice that should be at the center of how we form ourselves as teachers.

There is a danger, however, that the work of hospitality could be viewed as "nice" or lacking in a critical awareness of the conflicts and struggles of multicultural settings. Nothing could be further from the truth. In fact, genuine hospitality can sometimes be draining or taxing. That is, offering hospitality gives a person the right to make a claim on the one offering hospitality.[5] Thus, when I offer hospitality, I am required to put my own needs aside for the moment and attend to another.

Creating an open community of learners respectful of difference and honoring the pluralism of our world is a goal of multicultural teaching. The hospitality we seek to create is a form of attentiveness, for it requires of us receptivity to those with whom we interact.[6] When we are receptive to others, we attend to their distinctiveness, seeking to see them as person and not object. The development of a critical mind and a discerning heart demands receptivity to the complexity of the lives that students bring into the classroom with them. It demands receptivity to the ways in which that distinctiveness must become part of how and what we teach.

The vocational call to teach in multicultural settings involves attentiveness to God's creation in all of its intricacy, a hospitable openness, and engagement with the complexity of human community. This is our task and our joy as teachers. May God bless us with the will and the way to face this labor of love.

Notes

Introduction

[1]"Somewhere, on the edge of consciousness, there is what I call a *mythical norm*, which each of us in our hearts knows 'that is not me.' In America, this norm is usually defined as white, thin, male, young, heterosexual, christian, and financially secure." Audre Lorde, *Sister Outsider* (Trumansburg, N.Y.: The Crossing Press, 1984), 116.

[2]See Mary C. Boys, "A Word About Teaching Justly," and Thomas Groome, "Religious Education for Justice by Educating Justly," both in *Education for Peace and Justice,* ed. Padraic O'Hare (San Francisco: Harper and Row, 1983).

[3]For further discussion of this idea see Kathleen T. Talvacchia, "A Theoretical Framework for Multicultural Religious Education," *Horizons* 24, no. 2 (Fall 1997).

[4]Parker J. Palmer, *The Courage to Teach* (San Francisco: Jossey-Bass, 1998), 2.

[5]Ibid., 10.

[6]Ibid., 4–5.

[7] Some helpful texts that provide an overview of the multicultural education perspective are the following: James A. Banks, *Cultural Diversity and Education: Foundations, Curriculum, and Teaching*, 4th ed. (Boston: Allyn & Bacon, 2001); Christine I. Bennett, *Comprehensive Multicultural Education: Theory and Practice,* 4th ed. (Boston: Allyn & Bacon, 1999); Sonia Nieto, *Affirming Diversity: The Sociopolitical Context of Multicultural Education*, 2d ed. (White Plains, N.Y.: Longman Publishers, 1996); Leonard Davidman and Patricia T. Davidman, *Teaching with a Multicultural Perspective: A Practical Guide*, 3d ed. (New York: Addison-Wesley, 2001); James A. Banks and Cherry A. McGee Banks, eds., *Handbook of Research on Multicultural Education* (New York: Macmillan, 1995).

[8]Bennett, *Comprehensive Multicultural Education,* 11.

[9]Diana L. Eck, *Encountering God* (Boston: Beacon Press, 1993), 190–99.

[10]Ibid., 191.

[11]Ibid., 192.

[12]bell hooks, *Teaching to Transgress: Education as the Practice of Freedom* (New York: Routledge, 1994), 15.

[13]For works considering these issues from a church community perspective see Eric H. F. Law, *The Wolf Shall Dwell with the Lamb: A Spirituality for Leadership in a Multicultural Community* (St. Louis: Chalice Press, 1993); and Law, *Inclusion: Making Room for Grace* (St. Louis: Chalice Press, 2000).

[14]Stephen Brookfield, *The Skillful Teacher* (San Francisco: Jossey-Bass, 1990), 31.

[15]For more about critical incidents see Stephen Brookfield, "Using Critical Incidents to Explore Assumptions," in Jack Mezirow and Associates, *Fostering Critical Reflection in Adulthood* (San Francisco: Jossey-Bass, 1990); and Brookfield, *Developing Critical Thinkers* (San Francisco: Jossey-Bass, 1987), 97–109.

[16]For helpful discussions of the place of the action and reflection process in teaching see Thomas H. Groome, *Sharing Faith: A Comprehensive Approach to Religious Education and Pastoral Ministry: The Way of Shared Praxis* (San Francisco: Harper San Francisco, 1991); Donald Schön, *The Reflective Practioner* (New York: Basic Books, 1983); and Schön, *Educating the Reflective Practioner* (San Francisco: Jossey-Bass, 1987).

[17]Athena Gassoumis, Fall 1998, Union Theological Seminary.

[18]For useful resources on pedagogical design see Jane Vella, *Learning to Listen, Learning to Teach* (San Francisco: Jossey-Bass, 1994); and Lee Shulman, "Knowledge and Teaching: Foundations of the New Reform," *Harvard Educational Review* 57, no. 1 (February 1987).

Chapter 1: Perceptive Attentiveness

[1]This experience occurred before the publication of Margaret Guider's book *Daughters of Rahab: Prostitution and the Church of Liberation in Brazil* (Minneapolis: Fortress Press: 1995).

[2]I am obviously influenced in this thinking by Freire's important critique of what he refers to as the banking concept of education: "Narration (with the teacher as the narrator) leads the students to memorize mechanically the narrated content. Worse yet, it turns them into 'containers', into 'receptacles' to be filled by the teacher…Education thus becomes an act of depositing, in which the students are the depositories and the teacher is the depositor. Instead of communicating, the teacher issues communiqués and makes deposits which the students patiently receive, memorize, and repeat. This is the 'banking' concept of education, in which the scope of action allowed to the students extends only so far as receiving, filing, and storing the deposits." Paulo Freire, *Pedagogy of the Oppressed,* rev. ed. (New York: Continuum, 1993), 52–53.

[3]I am influenced in this understanding by Mary Boys' articulation of education as the process of making knowledge accessible: "Religious Education is the making accessible of the traditions of the religious community and the making manifest of the intrinsic connection between traditions and transformation." Mary C. Boys, *Educating in Faith* (San Francisco: Harper and Row, 1989), 193.

[4]Joe Holland and Peter Henriot, SJ, *Social Analysis: Linking Faith and Justice* (Maryknoll, N.Y.: Orbis Books, 1983), 14.

[5]Pepi Leistyna and Arlie Woodrum state, "Critical pedagogy…challenges us to recognize, engage, and critique (so as to transform) any existing undemocratic social practices and institutional structures that produce and sustain inequalities and oppressive social identities and social relations…Contrary to common misconceptions of critical pedagogy as a monolithic *discourse*, that is, one particular way of seeing the world—the vast literature and positions…demonstrate that not only are there multiple versions, but there is also no generic definition that can be applied to the term…Critical pedagogy is primarily concerned with the kinds of educational theories and practices that encourage both students and teachers to develop an understanding of the interconnecting relationship among ideology, power, and culture." Pepi Leistyna and Arlie Woodrum, "Context and Culture: What Is Critical Pedagogy?" in *Breaking Free: The Transformative Power of Critical Pedagogy,* ed. Pepi Leistyna, Arlie Woodrum, and Stephen A. Sherblom (Cambridge, Mass.: Harvard University Press, 1996), 2–3.

[6]The following texts are useful for understanding critical pedagogy: Stephen D. Brookfield, *Becoming a Critically Reflective Teacher* (San Francisco: Jossey-Bass, 1995); Henry A. Giroux and Peter McLaren, *Between Borders: Pedagogy and the Politics of Cultural Studies* (New York: Routledge, 1994); Barry Kanpol, *Critical Pedagogy: An Introduction,* 2d ed. (Westport, Conn.: Bergin and Garvey, 1999); Thomas S. Popkewitz and Lynn Fendler, eds., *Critical Theories in Education: Changing Terrains of Knowledge and Politics* (New York: Routledge, 1999); Carmen Luke, ed., *Feminisms and Pedagogies of Everyday Life* (Albany: SUNY Press, 1996); Patricia H. Hinchey, *Finding Freedom in the Classroom: A Practical Introduction to Critical Theory* (New York: Peter Lang, 1998); and Leistyna, Woodrum, and Sherblom, eds., *Breaking Free.*

[7]Thich Nhat Hanh, *The Miracle of Mindfulness* (Boston: Beacon Press, 1987), 11.

[8]For a helpful discussion on the term *solidarity,* see Michael A. Kelly, "Solidarity: A Foundational Educational Concern," *Religious Education* 93, no. 1 (Winter 1998).

[9]For more on compassion, see Matthew Fox, *A Spirituality Named Compassion* (New York: Harper and Row, 1979); Henri J. Nouwen, Donald P. McNeill, and Douglas A. Morrison, *Compassion* (New York: Doubleday/Image Books, 1982).

[10]Who decides what constitutes empowerment? Thus, it is important to note that while learner empowerment is an important goal of education, it must be subjected to critical questioning. See Elizabeth Ellsworth, "Why Doesn't This Feel Empowering? Working Through Repressive Myths of Critical Pedagogy," *Harvard Educational Review* 59, no. 3; Jennifer Gore, "What Can We *Do* For You! What *Can* We Do For You? Struggling Over Empowerment in

Critical and Feminist Pedagogies," *Educational Foundations* 4, no. 3: 5–26; Carmen Luke and Jennifer Gore, eds., *Feminisms and Critical Pedagogy* (New York: Routledge, 1992).

[11]Brookfield, *Developing Critical Thinkers.*

[12]Ibid., 7–9.

[13]Brookfield, *Becoming a Critically Reflective Teacher,* 10.

[14]Patricia A. Sakurai, " 'Just What Do I Think I'm Doing?' Enactments of Identity and Authority in the Asian American Literature Classroom," in *Teaching Asian America: Diversity and the Problem of Community,* ed. Lane Ryo Hirabayashi (New York: Rowman and Littlefield, 1998), 38.

[15]Denise Dombkowski Hopkins, Sharon H. Ringe, and Frederick C. Tiffany, "Reading the Bible in Global Context: Issues in Methodology and Pedagogy," in *Teaching the Bible: The Discourses and Politics of Biblical Pedagogy,* ed. Fernando F. Segovia and Mary Ann Tolbert (Maryknoll, N.Y.: Orbis Books, 1998), 312–13.

Chapter 2: Listening and Understanding

[1]Theological Institutional Partnership Consultation, Morija, Lesotho, January 12–16, 1998. Sponsored by the Division of Overseas Ministries, Christian Church (Disciples of Christ) and the United Church Board for World Ministries, United Church of Christ.

[2]Terry Provance, Common Global Ministries Board, report on the consultation.

[3]Cherríe Moraga, "La Guera," in *This Bridge Called My Back,* ed. Cherríe Moraga and Gloria Anzaldúa (New York: Kitchen Table, Women of Color Press, 1983), 29.

[4]Ibid.

[5]Ibid., 29–30.

[6]Merle Woo, "Letter to Ma," in Moraga and Anzaladúa, *This Bridge Called My Back,* 143.

[7]Minnie Bruce Pratt, "Identity: Skin Blood Heart," in *Yours in Struggle: Three Feminist Perspectives on Anti-Semitism and Racism,* ed. Elly Bulkin, Minnie Bruce Pratt, and Barbara Smith (Ithaca, N.Y.: Firebrand, 1988), 35.

[8]Ibid., 27.

[9]Laurent A. Parks Daloz, Cheryl H. Keen, James P. Keen, and Sharon Daloz Parks, *Common Fire: Leading Lives of Commitment in a Complex World* (Boston: Beacon Press, 1996), 72–74.

[10]John Haughey, "Hindsight Prayer and Compassion," in *Living with Apocalypse,* ed. Tilden H. Edwards (New York: Harper and Row, 1984), 134.

[11]Jace Weaver, "Native Americans and Religious Education," in *Multicultural Religious Education,* ed. Barbara Wilkerson (Birmingham, Ala.: Religious Education Press, 1997), 256–57.

[12]Nelle Morton, *The Journey Is Home* (Boston: Beacon Press, 1985), 55.

[13]Walter M. Abbott, ed., *The Documents of Vatican II* (New York: America Press, 1996).

[14]Richard P. McBrien, *Catholicism* (New York: HarperCollins, 1994), 95.

[15]Jane Vella, *Learning to Listen, Learning to Teach* (San Francisco: Jossey-Bass, 1994), 48–51.

Chapter 3: Seeing Clearly

[1]bell hooks has an interesting discussion of conflict, essentialism, and experience in an educational context and its role in identity-based classroom conversation. See bell hooks, *Teaching to Transgress* (New York: Routledge, 1994), 77–92.

[2]I am, of course, deeply influenced on this point by Beverly W. Harrison, who states, "Anger is—and it always is—a sign of some resistance in ourselves to the moral quality of the social relations in which we are immersed. Extreme and intense anger signals a deep reaction to the action upon us or toward others to whom we are related." From "The Power of Anger in the Work of Love," in Beverly W. Harrison, *Making the Connections,* ed. Carol S. Robb (Boston: Beacon Press, 1985), 14.

[3]For a discussion on cultural codes and anger in the classroom see bell hooks, *Feminist Theory: From Margin to Center* (Boston: South End Press, 1984), 56–57.

Chapter 4 : Acting Differently

[1]For a helpful discussion of the role of cognitive dissonance in adult learning see John M. Hull, *What Prevents Christian Adults from Learning?* (Philadelphia: Trinity Press International, 1991), 96–102, 123–43.

[2]Useful information and resources related to syllabus design and construction can be found in Barbara Gross Davis, *Tools for Teaching* (San Francisco: Jossey Bass, 1993), 14–19.

[3]For a helpful resource on varieties of teaching strategies see Bruce Joyce and Marsha Weil, *Models of Teaching,* 5th ed. (Boston: Allyn and Bacon, 1996).

Conclusion

[1]Ana María Pineda, "Hospitality," in *Practicing Our Faith,* ed. Dorothy C. Bass (San Francisco: Jossey Bass, 1997), 29–42.

[2]N. Lynne Westfield, *Dear Sisters: A Womanist Practice of Hospitality* (Cleveland: The Pilgrim Press, 2001), 48.

[3]Ibid., 49–52.

[4]Resource and Information Center for Empowerment (RICE), "Christian Practices of the Korean American Faith Community," unpublished, 2001, 120–29.

[5]I am indebted to Wesley Ariarajah from Drew Theological School for this insight. He made this point at a faculty workshop on multicultural teaching that I facilitated in March 2002.

[6]As Maria Harris points out, "Receptivity means bringing our receptive powers to bear on whatever reality lies before us—whether person or thing—and facing that reality as a 'Thou'." Maria Harris, *Fashion Me a People* (Louisville: Westminster/John Knox Press, 1989), 86-87.